# *Motivating Readers in the Middle Grades*

*Joan Collins*

**Linworth Books**

Professional Development Resources for K-12
Library Media and Technology Specialists

**Dedication**

To my family Brian, Mark, Gordon, and Noreen

Library of Congress Cataloging-in-Publication Data

Collins, Joan, 1946-
  Motivating readers in the middle grades / Joan Collins.
     p. cm.
  Includes bibliographical references and index.
  ISBN-13: 978-1-58683-297-1 (pbk.)
  ISBN-10: 1-58683-297-2 (pbk.)
  1.  Reading (Middle school) 2.  Reading promotion. 3.  Middle school students--Books and reading.  I. Title.
  LB1632.C575 2008

                    2007051426

Cynthia Anderson: Editor
Carol Simpson: Editorial Director
Judi Repman: Consulting Editor

Published by Linworth Publishing, Inc.
3650 Olentangy River Road
Suite 250
Columbus, Ohio 43214

ISBN 13: 978-1-58683-297-1
ISBN 10: 1-58683-297-2

5 4 3 2 1

# Table Of Contents

# Table Of Figures

# About the Author

Joan Collins is the teacher librarian at John Glenn Middle School in Bedford, Massachusetts. She has served as part-time faculty for Cambridge College in the library program. Before becoming a Massachusetts librarian, Joan worked as a high school librarian and as a junior high school English teacher in New York City. She was awarded the "Progressive School Library Media Award" in 1998 by Winnebago Software Company and has presented workshops for the Massachusetts School Library Association and for the New England League of Middle Schools. She has also reviewed software for *The Book Report*.

Joan is committed to sharing her enthusiasm for children's literature and her summer reading list can be viewed at *<www.bedford.k12.ma.us>*.

# Acknowledgments

This book would not have been written without the cooperation of key people on the staff of the John Glenn Middle School. When librarians collaborate with teachers, great things happen.

When we began reading motivation in 2003, the enthusiasm of Sarah Crosby and Marcia Marlow gave flight to Battle of the Books. Seventh grade teachers Lynda McGraw and Pat Stephen helped create Reading Playoffs. Eighth grade teachers Marilyn Bemis and Suzanne Alberich believed in Booked Conversation and encouraged their students to participate.

Without my assistant, Twila Wanamaker, who assists me in every way, there would be no book. I owe her all my gratitude and special thanks. She was and is both my right and left hand.

I owe special recognition to Judy Sima who inspired me at her workshop at AASL, which was my "ah ha" moment. Because of Judy, I took a risk and changed the reading culture at our school.

Finally, thanks to my companions in the land of story, Doris Smith and Jane Ruddock.

# Introduction

**Part One: Motivating the Reader**

Part One details three reading motivation programs – Battle of the Books, Reading Playoffs, and Booked Conversation – as well as author visits and how to use technology to pique student interest with books and to spark book discussion. Because they will have read many of the same titles, students will share a common literary experience. Books utilized have proven popularity with students in the middle grades.

**Part Two: Recommended Collection for Middle School**

Part Two features the recommended collection for middle school categorized into eight genres: adventure, contemporary issues, science fiction and fantasy, historical fiction, multicultural stories, mysteries, sports fiction, and nonfiction and biography. For 30 years, I have read children's books with pleasure and have discussed them with my readers and colleagues. I've led book discussion groups as part of Teachers as Readers. These book lists reflect my enthusiasm about these titles. I often think of them as the books no one ever complains about. I know that students will respond positively to them. I believe these books have literary merit and have sustained popularity. The included genres reflect varied interest and reading skills. These books can serve as a guide and starting point to connect with students and to support their burgeoning reading habit, books that students pronounce as really good.

PART
**ONE**

# *Motivating the Reader*

Using three different reading motivation programs, you will orchestrate a change in the reading culture in middle school. Starting with sixth grade, you will energize students with a reading competition, your version of Battle of the Books. Seventh graders will want to do battle again because they read together, competed together, and celebrated together. Middle schoolers enjoy reading when it is coupled with teamwork and competition. Isn't that what we want?

Knowing what young teens like to read will help construct the book lists for Battle of the Books, Reading Playoffs, and Booked Conversation. Knowing what teenagers like to read is key to selecting book lists for these programs. Book lists must offer compelling fiction and nonfiction that will hook readers into the world of story. These are the tried and true books that teenagers report are "really good." Tell your patrons no one complains about these books. They are winners.

Technology offers the opportunity to showcase books. Video booktalks will let students create their own booktalks and watch themselves and their friends promote hot titles online. Teenagers will be attracted to performing before the camera and incorporate book discussion into computer format.

This book will be a toolkit for motivating readers and starting conversation around books and reading. Students will take pride in reading and you will create lifelong lovers of reading. You will have sparked a dialogue that will nurture the reading environment. You will have created a culture around books and reading. The conversation is about books.

**CHAPTER ONE**

# Reading = Success

Many of us in our profession become librarians because we love books and reading. We want to share the joy of a good book and create lifelong lovers of books and reading. We remember our own childhoods often filled with classic folktales, terrific mysteries, and adventures, both real and imagined.

The good news is that love of story still thrives. All children still love to read and be read to by others. Magic still exists in books that capture the mind and imagination. The love of story is timeless.

In middle school, we hope to continue the process begun at an earlier age. If children already love reading, our task will be easier. We only need to be able to supply more of what they want. If by sixth grade, a student loves Matt Christopher books, then we will move him into Dan Gutman's time travel books or to such titles as *Danger Zone* or *Travel Team*. If Gail Carson Levine's *Ella Enchanted* is the ticket for the girls, *Goose Girl* and *Zel* are waiting in the wings.

For students who have not been exposed to books by parents or who have not had librarians at the elementary level, the task will be tougher. We need to hook students into reading at the middle school level. High school may be too late for many to get interested in books and reading. Just as children's books often tender breathtaking fantasies, teenage books speak to young adult concerns such as dating, fitting in, bullying, and family conflicts. When the subject of bullying comes up, you can hand the student James Howe's *The Misfits. P.S. Longer Letter Later* is a great read for anyone who has a best friend. *Life in the Fat Lane* will comfort someone who is overweight and *Slot Machine* will reassure some that athletics isn't for everyone.

Students may learn for the first time the pleasure of free choice in books and how agreeable that can be. If you encourage language arts teachers to assign free choice for book reports, rather than a specific genre, students are more likely to be matched with their interests and enjoy reading. If the student does not like science fiction, reading it can be a negative experience.

What we do know is that when children read freely and develop the reading habit, their academic achievement will improve. Stephen D. Krashen in his book, *The Power of Reading*, makes a persuasive argument that free voluntary reading (FVR) produces the highest levels of academic competence when students read for pleasure. Reading comprehension will improve, and following on that, writing, spelling, and vocabulary skills will increase.

Krashen values all school free reading programs (2-3). Many schools have sustained silent reading programs where teachers and students read for about 15 minutes a day. Tests have shown that there is no difference between free reading programs vs. traditional programs in terms of literary growth.

As a matter of fact, Krashen makes a compelling argument that free voluntary reading is more effective than direct instruction (18). Students can become thoroughly competent without learning an abundance of rules since language is too complex to learn a rule at a time. Formal instruction is not necessary for competence. Direct instruction delivers small impact. Krashen does not deal with students with learning difficulties who require special instruction, however.

As a librarian, finding books for reluctant readers can be a thorny task. Supplying the right title is so much more fulfilling for reluctant readers who think they hate reading. Librarians and teachers live for the words, "That was the best book!"

What most of us know in our hearts has been verified. Reading for pleasure is a joy, but it is also the best activity to promote language development. Three different studies, Bailey (1969), Grog (1969), and Greavy (1970) show that students prefer free voluntary reading to traditional pedagogy (Krashen 30).

In 1992, data reported by NAEP confirmed this philosophy. Grades 4, 8, and 12 were tested. The report concluded that "At all three grades, students who reported reading more frequently for pleasure on their own time had higher average reading proficiency than those who reported reading less frequently" (Mullis 11). Once again there is tremendous evidence to have children continue to enjoy the pleasure of reading.

Kathryn Edmunds and Kathryn Bauserman (February 2006) accepted the data that free voluntary reading had a positive effect on achievement (423).

They conducted a study with fourth graders set up as a conversational interview. They found what we librarians discover when questioning patrons about book choice. Children choose books that have action-packed plots. They respond to compelling book covers, scary titles, or the possibility of humor. Key here is that the young person is making the choice.

Once again, the school library plays a vital role. "Children overwhelmingly reported that they found out about their books from the school library" (419). School libraries were more important than classroom or public libraries. Librarians know what young people like to read.

Of the five conclusions Edmunds and Bauserman draw, they determine that librarians and the school library directly increase the motivation for students to read. Teacher/librarians note that poor reading attitudes often originate in middle school. Enthusiastic first graders can become negative sixth graders.

Ludo Verhoeven and Catherine Snow (2001) found, "As motivation declines, without promotional activities, children are less likely to read" (161-163).

What can we do? As we meet these new sixth graders, how can we rekindle the love of story or continue a reading habit already established?

We can provide enjoyable programs that create enthusiasm around books and reading. In Part One of my book, I will explain how to structure and implement these programs. Once the librarian gets the support of teachers and administrators, the culture of reading will prevail. You will be acknowledged as the authority on books.

Suddenly books will become as exciting as yesterday's soccer game.

# Works Cited

Edmunds, Kathryn M., and Kathryn Bauserman "What Teachers Can Learn about Reading Motivation through Conversations with Children." *The Reading Teacher* Feb. 2006: 414-424.

Krashen, Stephen D. *The Power of Reading Insights from the Research.* Portsmouth: Heinemann, 2004.

Mullis, Ina V. S., Jay R. Campbell, and Alan E. Farstrup. U.S. Data from the National and Trial State Assessments. National Center for Education Statistics. *NAEP 1992 Reading Report Card for the Nation and the States.* Washington, D.C.: Educational Testing Service, 1993.

Verhoeven, Ludo, and Catherine Snow. *Literacy and Motivation Reading Engagement in Individuals and Groups.* Mahwah: Lawrence Erlbaum Associates, 2001.

Motivating Readers in the Middle Grades

# *Battle of the Books*

Battle of the Books is not a new idea. It grew out of a Chicago radio program begun in 1938 (Kelly, xi). Two visionary women, Ruth Harshaw and Dilla MacBean, wanted to encourage reading by broadcasting a book contest on the radio over the local board of education station. Dilla was the hostess and Ruth was the questioner each Friday. School libraries provided questions, and school librarians also brought teams of students to the radio studio to compete. The show remained on the air for over 25 years. This proven concept continues to thrive and is as workable today as it was in the Forties. Librarians and teachers have adapted the program again and again. Battle of the Books is a compelling concept because teams of students read books and come together around them, but it is vital to fit the program to your individual school to guarantee success.

Students are challenged to read 10 books during a six-week period. They are grouped by classroom teachers to balance both strong and weak readers. Classmates hold each other responsible for reading the various titles, and enthusiasm is maintained throughout the six weeks by various contests. At the conclusion, a competition much like a spelling bee takes place and a winning team is crowned. Competition is a crafty approach to hooking middle schoolers into the reading process.

Battle of the Books is a complicated program, but with careful planning, the results will be quite satisfying. After a successful first year, you will continue to make modifications and find the variation that works best for you and your students.

## *STEP BY STEP*

### STEP ONE

#### Collaboration

Get together with teachers and discuss the books that will make up the Battle of the Books list. Ten titles is a good number. All of the books should be easy and enjoyable reads. Include bonus books for the high-powered readers. Book selection should be based on the kind of readers you have in your school community.

Books you choose should be available in paperback to protect your budget. The first year will be expensive, but books can be set aside for following years. In the second year when you evaluate your choices and re-plan, one or two titles may change. Plan on ordering about 24 copies per title, so there will be enough books for all the teams.

Teachers commit to placing students in teams of four, creating well-rounded groups of high and low readers. By second term, teachers know the reading levels in their classrooms and can group students in well-rounded teams.

Divide up the job of creating questions for the classroom and final battles with teachers. If you begin the program just prior to a school vacation week you allow students extra time to read.

- Select books
- Choose dates
- Divide up writing book questions

## Book Choices

Books should be easy reads to enable students to complete, if possible, the entire list. Try to avoid "girl" books or "boy" books. Select from different genres. There should be a mix of contemporary, mystery, historical fiction, and fantasy, and they should be short. A very workable list looks like this:

***The Watsons Go to Birmingham – 1963*** by Christopher Paul Curtis
> Readers will relate to the family dynamics of the Michigan family en route to Alabama and will get a healthy dose of both humor and history.

***Because of Winn-Dixie*** by Kate DiCamillo
> Here is an easy read where the dog does not die. Young children love the warm-hearted story of Opal and her dog, Winn-Dixie, set in Florida.

***Dovey Coe*** by Frances O'Roark Dowell
> A quick and suspenseful read where young readers will try to figure out "who done it." They will root for Dovey to win her case in court when she is accused of murder.

***Joey Pigza Swallowed the Key*** by Jack Gantos
> Jack Gantos knows those distractible students who are part of the school. The picture he creates of Joey, a boy with ADD, will resonate with students. Jack's heartfelt story is laden with humor and will grab the reader immediately.

***Mama, Let's Dance*** by Patricia Hermes
> Children's literature often eliminates the parents so that youngsters get to make big decisions usally executed by adults. *Mama, Let's Dance* tells the story of three children who try to hold their family together when they are deserted by their mother in this tearjerker for sixth grade.

***Which Witch?*** by Eva Ibbotson
> This entertaining fantasy from Eva Ibbotson is chock full of laughs. Even a non-fantasy reader will fall in love with goofy characters who blithely practice witchcraft.

***Transall Saga*** by Gary Paulsen
Gary Paulsen takes his survival fiction into the future. Readers who loved *Hatchet* will succumb to the story of Mark's adventure in another world.

***The View from the Cherry Tree*** by Willo Davis Roberts
In this tried and true mystery from Willo Davis Roberts, Rob admits seeing a murder, but no one believes him. The murderer knows Rob has witnessed an old woman fall from the window. Recognizable characters add to the contemporary story.

***Crash*** by Jerry Spinelli
Football and Quakers! Jerry Spinelli transforms Crash Cogan into a much nicer guy. From football jock to heartfelt youngster, Crash learns to respect others.

***The Dollhouse Murders*** by Betty Ren Wright
Amy Trefor will slowly uncover the clues to a family mystery. She will find out who committed the crime many years ago from the evidence in a dollhouse found in her aunt's attic.

## Preparation

Get ready to roll out the program by creating handouts for students. The first is a letter to parents explaining the program. Require that students have their parents sign and return the letter. Also, give students a description of the rules.

Additionally, create a bookmark listing the titles and authors of the Battle of the Books books. Students will appreciate this as they select books to read.

• Write parent letter < see Figure 2.1 >

• Create bookmarks < see Figure 2.2 >

• Timeline for students containing program description < see Figure 2.3 >

**HEAR YE! HEAR YE!**

The sixth graders at the _____ Middle School are now engaged in a battle!

**BATTLE OF THE BOOKS!**

During the next six weeks your child will take part in an exciting reading motivational program. Each student will be part of a team that will be responsible for reading as many books on the Battle list as possible. Students may earn extra points for their team by creating a team poster, carrying a Battle book and wearing a team outfit on Fridays, and returning this parent letter. There are 10 books in all. The books offer a variety of genre and reading levels.

After six weeks the teams will be asked questions about the books. Students will be asked to recall specific details from each book. The winning teams from each reading class will compete at a final tournament the week of _____. All sixth graders will be cheering for their team representatives. The winning team earns a pizza party for their class.

This communication is meant to enlist your support and ask that you encourage your child's reading efforts at home. Please sign the slip below and return it to your son or daughter's reading teacher.

Co-Coordinators of the Battle of the Books

_ _ _ _ _ _ _ _ _ _ _ _ _Tear Off_ _ _ _ _ _Return to School_ _ _ _ _ _ _ _ _ _ _ _ _ _ _ _ _

I acknowledge my child _____ is participating in the Battle of the Books.

Parent Signature_____

Figure 2.1: Parent Letter

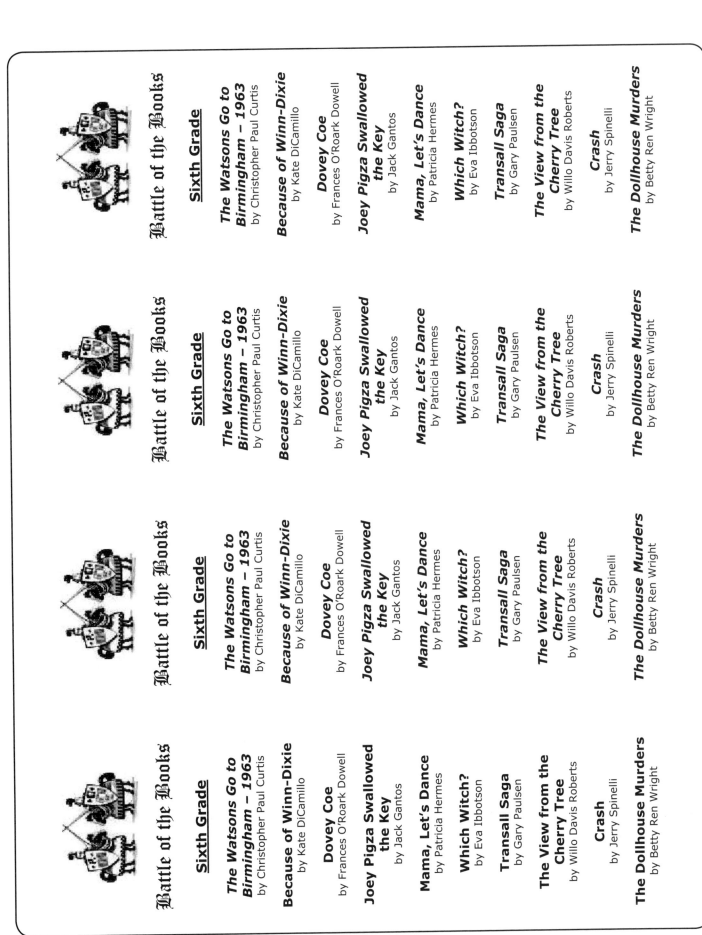

Figure 2.2: Bookmarks

**BATTLE OF THE BOOKS**
**THE CHARGE!**

During the next six weeks, students will be divided into teams of five or six students. To maintain a high level of interest, students will have approximately six weeks to read before the classroom battles begin. Reading teachers will bring the entire class to the library to check out the books for the first time. Students are to read as many of the Battle books as they can during the six weeks prior to the first tournament. At the end of six weeks, all classes will compete at the classroom level to send a team to participate in the final battle.

## CLASSROOM BATTLES

At the classroom battles, students are to be seated by team. One or two questions will be asked for each book on the list. As a team, students decide the best answer for the question. The team captain writes the answer along with the author's last name on a piece of paper. At the end of the class period, the points are added up. At that time, the extra points that the teams have earned are added to the score. A winning team will be selected from each learning group.

## FINAL BATTLE

The final grade-wide competition will take place with the winners from each classroom battle. The first place team members earn a pizza party for their entire class, and their names will be displayed in the library and announced over the PA system.

## BATTLE DUTIES
### Teacher Responsibility

Create teams of five or six students in your literature class. Each team needs a team name and a team captain. Please return one of the attached team lists for every team as soon as the teams are established. Teams should be established before the Captains' meeting. Parent letters explaining Battle of the Books should be sent home with each student to be signed, returned, and given to the team captain. A copy of the letter is attached.

### Team Captain's Responsibility

Keep track of the books read by your team members. The team captain also keeps track of the team's extra points. Every book on the list should be read by at least two team members. Students should memorize book titles and authors' last names in order to receive extra points during the classroom and final battles. Team posters need to be completed by _____.

### Student Responsibility

Read as many books as possible. Extra points can be earned through the following means:

### Extra Points

Teams may earn extra points, which will be added to their classroom battle score.

- *Parent letter* – one point per team member if he or she returns the parent letter signed. (Copy of letter is attached.)

- *Book check* – one point per team member for having your Battle book on Fridays. Book checks take place in the classrooms on Fridays.

- *Team poster* – 10 extra points per team given for creating a team poster. Posters may be turned in as soon as they are finished. All posters are due by _____. Judging will take place the next week. Coupons will be given for the best posters. One or more members of the team must make the poster. Any type of paper or materials may be used.

- *Team outfit* – five extra points given to teams that have some symbol identifying themselves as a team (e.g., a common hat or scarf or shirt) on Fridays only. For six weeks, Fridays will be designated as Book and Spirit Check Day.

*Let the battle begin!*

Figure 2.3: Program Description - The Charge

## Big Event

Gather the entire sixth grade in a large assembly room. As students take their seats, have a CD playing the Olympic march. Add to the drama of the moment. Dress up as medieval royalty brandishing swords and regale the students to "battle to win." That playacting will continue to churn up the excitement.

Booktalk the 10 titles, doing your best to promote interest in the stories themselves. Tell the participants what will be expected of them over the next six weeks, engaging them with promises of pizza parties and free ice cream. Distribute the handouts to the assembly of students.

- Plan for publicity by asking a teacher or student to take photos with a digital camera.
- Gather the entire grade
- Perform booktalks
- Describe program
- Give out handouts

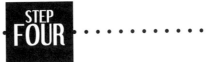

## Weekly Activities: Keep It Going

Classroom teachers will have already set up the teams of four or five students. One student should be designated as the team captain and will have the responsibility over the next six weeks to keep track of who has read each book on the list.

Teachers send students to the library to check out the books after each child selects a book to read. Circulation statistics will begin to climb. Shelve books for the Battle of the Books in a separate space, identified with Battle of the Books spine labels.

Teachers provide some classroom time for teams to create a team poster with a name and theme. These posters will be judged in different categories and teams will be awarded the first of many ice cream coupons. The coupons are redeemed at the school cafeteria during lunch period.

Fridays are designated for Book and Spirit Check, and will continue the bubble of enthusiasm. The teams decide on a simple costume. They might wear a local sports team shirt or identifying scarf or matching hats; students get very creative. The best outfits qualify for ice cream coupons or other motivators such as homework passes.

During those weeks, add on other contests to keep stimulating the fire such as designing bookmarks and crowns, creating posters, or writing raps. Winners will receive rewards.

Another option is to have the principal read questions from the books at lunchtime and award the winner an ice cream coupon while in the cafeteria.

Each Friday, visit classrooms where students will be eagerly waiting. Carry the omnipresent ice cream coupons and a digital camera to take pictures of all of the teams. Print and laminate them to create ideal "PR." What parent does not enjoy seeing his or her child's photo displayed? Students love walking by the display in the halls to see themselves pictured in costume. This further encourages the action and hoopla.

- Each Friday, do Book and Spirit Check with camera and rewards such as ice cream coupons
- Add on additional contests, e.g., bookmarks, crowns, rap writing
- Create hall photo displays
- Mark used questions to save others for the final tournament

# Battle of the Books

*Battle of the Books*
Team Name _____ Lit. Teacher_____

Team Captain_____

Team Members_____

_____

_____

_____

_____

_____

| Author | Title | Assigned to |
|---|---|---|
| Curtis | *The Watson's Go to Birmingham-1963* | |
| DiCamillo | *Because of Winn-Dixie* | |
| Dowell | *Dovey Coe* | |
| Gantos | *Joey Pigza Swallowed the Key* | |
| Hermes | *Mama, Let's Dance* | |
| Ibbotson | *Which Witch?* | |
| Paulsen | *Transall Saga* | |
| Roberts | *The View from the Cherry Tree* | |
| Spinelli | *Crash* | |
| Wright | *The Dollhouse Murders* | |

Points_____

Figure 2.4: Team Assignment Form

## Group Name _____

| **BONUS** | | | | | |
|---|---|---|---|---|---|
| The Dollhouse Murders | | | | | |
| Crash | | | | | |
| The View from the Cherry Tree | | | | | |
| Transall Saga | | | | | |
| Which Witch? | | | | | |
| Mama, Let's Dance | | | | | |
| Joey Pigza Swallowed the Key | | | | | |
| Dovey Coe | | | | | |
| Because of Winn-Dixie | | | | | |
| The Watsons Go to Birmingham - 1963 | | | | | |
| **Team Members** | | | | | |

■ Fill in entire box when a book is finished.

◪ Fill in half a box if a book is in progress.

Figure 2.5: Team Record Keeper

**ICE CREAM COUPON**

Date _____

Name_____

*Battle of the Books*

- - - - -     - - - -     - - - -     - - - -     - - - -     - - - - -

**ICE CREAM COUPON**

Date _____

Name_____

*Battle of the Books*

- - - - -     - - - -     - - - -     - - - -     - - - -     - - - - -

**ICE CREAM COUPON**

Date _____

Name_____

*Battle of the Books*

- - - - -     - - - -     - - - -     - - - -     - - - -     - - - - -

**ICE CREAM COUPON**

Date _____

Name_____

*Battle of the Books*

- - - - -     - - - -     - - - -     - - - -     - - - -     - - - - -

**ICE CREAM COUPON**

Date _____

Name_____

*Battle of the Books*

**ICE CREAM COUPON**

Date _____

Name_____

*Battle of the Books*

Figure 2.6: Ice Cream Coupons

# Battle of the Books

## PROJECT DETAILS

**Bookmark**

Standard bookmark size
Only one title per bookmark
Original artwork (Do not duplicate the cover of the book)
On back of bookmark, your name and team name

**Crown Contest**

Earn 10 points for your team.
Design a crown and wear it on Friday during Book and Spirit Check.

- Head sized
- Must be original
- Artwork may reflect any theme

**Poem or Rap**

10 lines per person (e.g., a group rap would mean 3 people = 30 lines)
Expresses theme, action from the plot, or characterization (e.g., for *Tears of a Tiger*, rap about the car crash)

Figure 2.7: Project Details

**Classroom Battles**

At the end of six weeks, students will compete within their classrooms to send a winning team to the final. Teams begin the contest with the points accumulated during the past six weeks. Students may choose to wear their costumes for the battle.

Ideally, the teacher and librarian should administer the playoffs. Distribute scrap paper to the teams and have them write their team names down on the paper. Tell the participants to decide who will record the answers and who will be the runner. The librarian will ask questions and the teacher will score the answers. Students may earn credit for the author's name as well as the correct answer. The winning team is decided at the end of the class period and will be psyched to move to the final competition.

• Bring questions and scrap paper to battles

# Sixth Grade Battle of the Books
### Questions & Answers for Classroom & Final Battles
*The Watsons Go to Birmingham -- 1963*
by Christopher Paul Curtis

1. **Who had his tongue stuck to a rear-view mirror?**
   Byron
2. **Where did the Watsons live?**
   Flint, Michigan
3. **What was the Brown Bomber?**
   Watson's car, a 1948 Plymouth
4. **What was wrong with Kenneth's eye?**
   Lazy eye
5. **Where were Rufus and Cody from?**
   Arkansas
6. **Why did Kenny stop hanging around with LJ Jones?**
   He stole his dinosaurs.
7. **Who was Joey?**
   The Watsons' youngest sibling (a daughter)
8. **Who stole Kenny's glove?**
   Larry Dunn
9. **What was Byron's favorite cookie?**
   Swedish crèmes
10. **After Byron killed the bird, what did he do with the carcass?**
    Buried it with Popsicle sticks as a cross and gave it a funeral
11. **What did Byron's father do to him after he colored and straightened his hair?**
    Shaved it

12. **Why did the Watsons go to Birmingham?**

> To visit Grandma Sands and leave Byron there for the summer for some home training

13. **Who was Buphead?**

> Byron's best friend

14. **What was Kenny's favorite record?**

> Yakety Yak

15. **What was Mr. Robert's dog's name?**

> Toddy

16. **Where did Grandma Sands tell the Watson kids not to go to because it is dangerous?**

> Collier's Landing

17. **Who is the person that wanted to cross the "Warning No Trespassing! No Swimming! No Public Entry!" sign?**

> Kenny

18. **Who is Winnie-the-Pooh's twin brother?**

> Wool Pooh

19. **As Kenny was drowning, who did he see in his mind?**

> Joetta, the little angel

20. **Who saved Kenny from the whirlpool?**

> Byron

21. **What was the loud noise Kenny heard while sleeping under the old magnolia tree?**

> The church blowing up

22. **What did Kenny take from the church after it was blown up?**

> Shiny black shoe and frilly white sock

23. **Who did Kenny think took Joey at the bombing?**

> Wool Pooh

24. **How many little girls were killed during the church bombing?**

> Four

25. **Why did Joey get upset with Kenny after the bombing?**

> She thought Kenny took her shoe and/or he was acting weird.

26. **What is Kenny's complete name?**

> Kenneth Bernard Watson

27. **Where was Kenny's secret hiding place at home?**

> Behind the couch

28. **After the bombing, about whom were the Watson parents most worried?**

> Kenny

29. **What was Kenny's secret hiding place called?**

> World-Famous Watson Pet Hospital

30. **Who bombed the church? Why?**

> Two white men. Hatred.

# Sixth Grade Battle of the Books
## Questions & Answers for Classroom & Final Battles
*Because of Winn-Dixie*
by Kate DiCamillo

1.  **Why did the preacher call India by her middle name, Opal?**
    Because Opal was his mother's first name
2.  **What kind of store is Winn-Dixie?**
    Grocery store, supermarket
3.  **Why did Opal feel like an orphan?**
    Her mother left her when she was three years old.
4.  **What did Gloria Dump and Opal call the tree they planted?**
    A wait-and-see tree
5.  **How did Winn-Dixie behave during a storm?**
    He became very fearful and ran around the house.
6.  **What happened to the animals when Otis played his guitar?**
    They listened and looked like stone.
7.  **Why did Gloria Dump have a ghost tree?**
    For the things that she had done wrong in her life
8.  **Littmus Black, Miss Franny's great-grandfather, had fought in what war?**
    The Civil War
9.  **What made Littmus wealthy?**
    He built a candy factory and sold Littmus Lozenges.
10. **What was the secret ingredient in the Littmus Lozenge?**
    Sorrow
11. **Why did Opal say that a Littmus Lozenge was like life?**
    Because sweet and sad were all mixed together and it was hard to separate them
12. **What book did Opal begin to read to Gloria Dump?**
    Gone with the Wind
13. **What character had spent time in jail?**
    Otis
14. **Who planned the party with Opal?**
    Gloria Dump
15. **What did Sweetie Pie Thomas bring to the party?**
    Pictures of dogs
16. **What did Otis bring to the party?**
    A jar of pickles
17. **Why was the party moved inside?**
    It began to rain.
18. **Where did Winn-Dixie go during the storm?**
    In Gloria Dump's room under her bed
19. **Why was the "list of 10 things" important to Opal?**
    To help her remember her mother
20. **Who was the town librarian?**
    Miss Franny Block

# Sixth Grade Battle of the Books
## Questions & Answers for Classroom & Final Battles
*Dovey Coe*
by Frances O'Roark Dowell

1. **Where did Dovey and her family live?**
   Indian Creek, North Carolina
2. **How many siblings does Dovey have?**
   Two (sister Caroline and brother Amos)
3. **What was the name of Parnell's sister?**
   Paris
4. **What did Caroline want to do after high school?**
   She wanted to be a teacher in Charlotte, Raleigh, or Asheville.
5. **What is the name of the Parnell family store?**
   Caraway Dry Goods
6. **Both Paris and Dovey wanted to travel out of the country. Where did they want to go?**
   London, England
7. **Who killed Parnell Caraway?**
   Amos Coe
8. **What caused Amos' deafness?**
   Water on his brain
9. **How did Mrs. Coe call her children home for dinner?**
   She rang the dinner bell.
10. **What were the names of Amos' dogs?**
    Tom and Huck
11. **What did Parnell initially say to Dovey about Amos that made her hate him?**
    Parnell called Amos a "monkey."
12. **What musical instrument did Mr. Coe play?**
    Guitar
13. **What did Caroline want to be instead of Mrs. Parnell Caraway?**
    A teacher
14. **What decoration idea did Amos have for the party to make it look festive?**
    Multicolored paper chains
15. **How old is Dovey?**
    12 years old
16. **What did Dovey call her grandparents?**
    MeMaw and Pawpaw
17. **What did Dovey say was the most difficult concept to explain to Amos?**
    Sound of music
18. **Who did Dovey hold hands with at the party?**
    Wilson Brown
19. **What question does Parnell ask Caroline in front of the entire community?**
    Will you marry me?
20. **Which lawyer was hired to defend Dovey?**
    Mr. Thomas G. Harding

# Sixth Grade Battle of the Books

**Questions & Answers for Classroom & Final Battles**

*Joey Pigza Swallowed the Key*

by Jack Gantos

1. **Name the town where Joey's father lives.**
   Pittsburgh
2. **What other family members does Joey claim are wired?**
   Father and grandfather
3. **Grandma threatens to punish Joey. In what appliance does she tell Joey he will be placed?**
   Refrigerator
4. **Where does the school ask Joey's mother to take him before he starts school in the fall?**
   Doctor
5. **What distracts Joey so he cannot listen to Mrs. Maxy?**
   Red nail polish
6. **What nickname have the neighborhood children given Joey?**
   Zippy
7. **What does Seth Justman promise Joey if he swallows his house key?**
   One dollar
8. **Where does Mrs. Howard place Joey to see how long he can sit still?**
   Big Quiet Chair
9. **What does Joey get from Mrs. Howard when he kicks the legs of the chair?**
   Fuzzy bunny slippers
10. **Yes or no...Does Joey's mother think her drinking is related to Joey's behavioral problem?**
    No
11. **Where do the fourth and fifth grade classes go on a field trip?**
    Amish farm
12. **What does Mrs. Maxy give Joey as a substitute for a shoofly pie?**
    Apple slice
13. **What does Joey take from Mrs. Maxy without permission?**
    Scissors
14. **How long will Joey be suspended for hurting another student?**
    Six weeks
15. **What breed of dog does Joey want?**
    Chihuahua
16. **What is Mr. Ed Vanness' nickname?**
    Special Ed
17. **What is a brain SPECT test?**
    X-ray of the brain
18. **What trouble does Joey cause in the hospital gift shop?**
    Spins the postcard rack
19. **What does Joey name the dog?**
    Pablo
20. **Who does Joey invite to visit his dog?**
    Charlie

# Sixth Grade Battle of the Books
## Questions & Answers for Classroom & Final Battles
*Mama, Let's Dance*
by Patricia Hermes

1.  **Why is it that Ariel, Mary Belle, and Callie did not have any relatives to contact when Mama left?**
    Both of their parents were "only" children.
2.  **What type of garden did Mama keep?**
    Vegetable garden or kitchen garden
3.  **What was the name of the man who came to check on the garden and became suspicious of where mother was?**
    Amarius
4.  **About how old was Amarius?**
    People thought he was about 90 years old.
5.  **What color dress did the May Queen wear?**
    White
6.  **Who picks the May Queen?**
    School people make the decision.
7.  **Who is Mary Belle's best friend at school?**
    Anna Telby
8.  **What happened to Mary Belle's father?**
    He was killed in a mining accident.
9.  **What is the name of the creek that passes through the road to Callie, Mary Belle, and Ariel's house?**
    Narrow Passage Creek
10. **What type of job did Ariel have to make money to pay the bills?**
    Worked at a gas station
11. **At Mary Belle's family's first dinner, what did Amarius bring?**
    Fried chicken
12. **When does Mary Belle realize that Callie has lost a lot of weight in a just a few weeks?**
    When Mary Belle puts Callie's May Queen dress on
13. **When did the May Fair take place?**
    The last day of school in the afternoon
14. **What does Mama ask Ariel to do in the letter that she sent him?**
    Send her $50.00 for a new dancing dress
15. **Who helped Mary Belle call the doctor and take Callie to the hospital?**
    Miss Dearly
16. **Who became Ariel and Mary Belle's foster parents?**
    Amarius and Miss Dearly
17. **Why did Mary Belle run away from the hospital?**
    She did not want to hear the news about Callie that made Amarius cry.
18. **What did Mary Belle pick out for Callie to wear when she was buried?**
    A dancing dress, her May Queen dress
19. **Who did Mama tell that she was not coming home?**
    Corley

20. **What was Callie's dog's name?**
    Miss Mannie
21. **What does Mary Belle write?**
    Songs
22. **What was the last thing that Mary Belle said to Callie?**
    I love you.
23. **How long do Ariel and Mary Belle have to stay in foster care?**
    At least one year, until Ariel turns 18

. . . . . . . . . . . . . . . . . . . . . . . . . . . . . . . . . . . . . . . . . . . . . .

# Sixth Grade Battle of the Books
### Questions & Answers for Classroom & Final Battles
*Which Witch?*
by Eva Ibbotson

1. **Mr. & Mrs. Canker noticed that their baby was born with an unusual physical characteristic. What was it?**
    Arriman was born with a full set of teeth.
2. **What was Arriman's original name?**
    He was called George.
3. **Sir Simon Montpelier, the Darkington ghost, was murdered by his wives. How many were there?**
    There were seven wives.
4. **How many eyes did Lester, the ogre, have?**
    He had only one eye.
5. **What did Esmeralda, the gypsy, predict to Arriman?**
    She said a great new wizard with great power would come and remove Arriman's burden.
6. **What made Mr. Leadbetter think he was a demon?**
    He was born with a small tail.
7. **What sort of animal was Mrs. Wrack's familiar?**
    Her familiar, Doris, was an octopus.
8. **Nancy and Nora Shouter were identical twins with dyed red hair and long noses who kept their familiars under the bed. What were they?**
    Chickens
9. **Mother Bloodwort often forgot her spells. What did she turn into?**
    A table
10. **Monolot, otherwise known as Gwendolyn Swamp, was ill with what disease?**
    Measles
11. **The competition to be Arriman's bride was to take place during what holiday?**
    Halloween
12. **What gift did Arriman leave the witches on the rock after announcing the contest?**
    Oval hand mirrors
13. **What creature suggests that Belladonna at least try to compete in the contest?**
    A bat from Belladonna's hair

14. **Madame Olympia arrived at the Grand Spa Hotel wearing a cape of puppy skin. What sort of necklace did she have?**

   A necklace of human teeth

15. **Where was Terence Mugg found as an abandoned baby?**

   Railway station

16. **What outfit were all the witches to wear for the competition?**

   Black gowns and hoods

17. **In what device did Terence carry Rover in his pocket?**

   In a matchbox

18. **In what did Mr. Chatterjee live most of the year?**

   A bottle (He was a genie.)

19. **What sort of person was Mr. Sniveler?**

   A ghoul

20. **Who always first appeared in the broom cupboard?**

   Sir Simon Montpelier

21. **There were two rules for the Ms. Witch of Todcaster. One was any witch practicing black magic on another witch would be disqualified. What was the second?**

   Competitors must not show their faces.

22. **What is kept in Davy Jones' locker?**

   Bodies of drowned sailors

23. **Who was Mabel Wrack going to call from the sea during the contest?**

   Kraker (a dangerous sea monster said to dwell in Norwegian waters)

24. **What score did Mabel Wrack earn in the contest?**

   Four

25. **Ethel Feedbag's trick involved three types of trees. One was an ash; one was an oak. What was the other type of tree?**

   Thorn or hawthorn

26. **Which of the Shouter sisters fell into the bottomless hall?**

   Nora

27. **Arriman planned to kill himself if what witch won the competition?**

   Mother Bloodwort (warts, whiskers, cloud of flies)

28. **What did Princess Juanita become during Mother Bloodwort's magic demonstration?**

   Lame duck instead of a black swan

29. **Who performed the Symphony of Death?**

   Madame Olympia

30. **When Madame Olympia laid the whip across the back of the aardvark and cracked her whip, what appeared?**

   Rats

31. **What Shakespearian role did Monty Moon previously play at Stratford?**

   Ghost in Hamlet

32. **What did Belladonna do at the end of her witchcraft demonstration after bringing Sir Simon to life?**

   She fainted.

33. **What does Belladonna call Arriman when she first meets him?**

   Arry

34. **Mugg the Magnificent was the future name of whom?**

   Terence

# Sixth Grade Battle of the Books

### Questions & Answers for Classroom & Final Battles
*Transall Saga*
by Gary Paulsen

1. **How long was Mark Harrison allowed to backpack?**
   Two weeks

2. **Why did Mark lose his balance and fall into the strange light?**
   A rattlesnake bit him.

3. **What did Mark find to help get out of the quicksand?**
   A root

4. **What did Mark name the strange, furry creature that showed him how to eat the tree rocks?**
   Willie

5. **How did Mark think he was going to return to the desert?**
   Find the blue light

6. **What did Mark learn from Willie about getting to the top of the trees?**
   Swing back and forth on the vines

7. **Why was his spear the best weapon?**
   It was long and straight and had a finely carved point.

8. **What was the significance of finding the arrow?**
   It had to be made by a human.

9. **Why did Mark decide to find the arrow people?**
   It was better than being alone.

10. **Mark compared the arrow people with what time period?**
    Prehistoric time

11. **Why did Mark decide to leave Leeta's village?**
    The people of the tribe were too different and they didn't care about wiping out the village.

12. **In trying to help Leeta when she injured her foot, how did Mark put his own life in danger?**
    By carrying her on his back

13. **After Mark successfully escaped from the Tsook people, why did he return?**
    The cannibals were going to attack Leeta's village.

14. **How did Mark have to show his loyalty to the Tsook?**
    He had to cut his palm and shake hands to mix his blood with the Tsook.

15. **What was unusual about Barow's gift to Mark, and what conclusion did he make?**
    It was a blue glass with Coca Cola stamped on it; therefore, Mark had to be on Earth.

16. **What were the other pieces of evidence to support Mark's conclusion?**
    Artifacts written with the following words: USAF, General Motors, made in Japan, and Pyrex

17. **Mark is used to being on his own. Sarbo joins him as they travel with the Merkon. Give three reasons why Paulsen needed to include Sarbo in this part of the story.**
    Sarbo knew the terrain, knew about Trisad, and would offer more protection.

18. **How did Mark's science knowledge help the escape from the Samatin camp?**
    Mark remembered what he needed to make an explosive using charcoal and potassium nitrate.

19. **The epilogue continues Mark's story many years later. Describe his research and the purpose of his study?**

He wants to find a cure for the Ebola virus so that he can save life from being destroyed in the future.

20. **What is the importance of the lab assistant's comment about Mark's savage look?**

   It could be proof that all of Mark's experiences really happened.

. . . . . . . . . . . . . . . . . . . . . . . . . . . . . . . . . . . . . . . . . . .

# Sixth Grade Battle of the Books
### Questions & Answers for Classroom & Final Battles
*The View from the Cherry Tree*
by Willo Davis Roberts

1. **How long had Rob lived next door to Mrs. Calloway?**
   Nine years
2. **How old was Rob?**
   11 years old
3. **Where was Rob's favorite place to be?**
   In the cherry tree
4. **Who was Darcy?**
   Rob's older sister
5. **What big event was occurring in the story?**
   Darcy's wedding
6. **Who were Max and Derek?**
   Old boyfriends of Darcy
7. **Why is it that Mrs. Calloway was not well liked?**
   Fussy, always complaining
8. **What did Mrs. Calloway usually wear around her neck?**
   Binoculars
9. **In what kind of trouble had Uncle Ray been involved?**
   Used $1,200,000 of his company's money illegally
10. **What caused Rob's black eye?**
   Mrs. Calloway hit him with a broom.
11. **What did Rob see from the cherry tree?**
   Mrs. Calloway's murder
12. **How did the rest of the family and the police think Mrs. Calloway died?**
   Accident, strangulation from binocular strap
13. **Why is it that Rob's mom and dad did not listen to Rob about what really happened to Mrs. Calloway?**
   Mom was too busy with wedding plans, and Dad left to take care of Uncle Ray.
14. **Who was the first person Rob told about the murder?**
   Derek
15. **Who was the second person Rob told about the murder?**
   Max
16. **What was the first attempt on Rob's life?**
   Someone shooting at him, three shells
17. **What was the second attempt on Rob's life?**
   Flower pot thrown at him

18. **Who died of food poisoning?**
    Siamese cat
19. **Who was the murderer?**
    Derek
20. **What did Rob throw at Derek's face to save himself?**
    Gigantic spider

. . . . . . . . . . . . . . . . . . . . . . . . . . . . . . . . . . . . . . . . . . . . . . . . . . .

# Sixth Grade Battle of the Books
### Questions & Answers for Classroom & Final Battles
*Crash*
by Jerry Spinelli

1. **For what event was Penn Webb named when he was born?**
    His great-grandfather named him after the Penn State track meet, Penn Relays.
2. **Why is it that Penn would not shoot the water gun at Crash?**
    He was a Quaker, and Quakers don't believe in violence.
3. **Crash thought that there were two unusual things about Penn's house. One was that it was the size of a garage; what was the other?**
    No TV
4. **Penn wore a button when he first met Crash that said, "I'm a flickertail." What is a flickertail?**
    Squirrel (North Dakota is called the Flickertail State.)
5. **Penn had two toys, a Conestoga wagon and dried mud from the Missouri River. What was the mud supposed to do?**
    Heal what is wrong with you after 50 years
6. **When Crash and his best friend, Mike Deluca, went out for football, what team did Penn try out for?**
    Cheerleading
7. **What was Crash's grandfather's job when he was a young man?**
    Cook in the U.S. Navy
8. **Who comes to live with Crash and his family?**
    Grandfather
9. **Who suffers a terrible stroke?**
    Grandfather
10. **What kind of pet did Scooter supposedly have when he was in the Navy?**
    Ollie, the one-armed Octopus
11. **What did Crash buy Scooter for Christmas when he thought that any present would keep him from dying?**
    Red high-heeled shoes
12. **What store did they come from?**
    Second Time Around resale shop
13. **What gift did Penn leave for Scooter after he had his stroke?**
    The jar of mud from the bottom of the Missouri River
14. **Why was Crash's mother upset when Abby joined the protesters to stop the building of the new mall?**
    Mother's real estate job was leasing stores for the mall.

15. **When Crash's mother dumped everything out of his football laundry bag, what came out the bag besides laundry?**
    A mouse
16. **What did Crash make for Abby's birthday because Scooter could not?**
    Catfish cakes
17. **What important event marked the beginning of Crash's change from being a bully?**
    Scooter's stroke
18. **Crash was good at football. What other sport did he excel at?**
    Running track
19. **At the book's conclusion, who wins the race?**
    Penn
20. **What did Crash yell to Penn when they were racing that helped Penn to win the race?**
    Lean

. . . . . . . . . . . . . . . . . . . . . . . . . . . . . . . . . . . . . . . . . . . . . . . . .

# *Sixth Grade Battle of the Books*
### Questions & Answers for Classroom & Final Battles
*The Dollhouse Murders*
by Betty Ren Wright

1. **Aunt Claire had been given the dollhouse as a birthday present for her fifteenth birthday. What had she wanted instead?**
   Record player
2. **What did Louann do at the mall that made the shore owner angry?**
   Picked the tulips from the pot
3. **Who or what tipped over the garbage cans at the old house?**
   Raccoons
4. **What year were Grandma and Grandpa murdered?**
   1952
5. **Where was Amy's father found when his grandparents were murdered?**
   Asleep in closet
6. **What happened to Claire's boyfriend the night of the Trelors' murder?**
   Died when car hit a tree
7. **Where was the dollhouse kept?**
   Attic
8. **How many dolls lived in the dollhouse?**
   4
9. **Which doll cried the night Louann and Amy went to the attic to see the lights in the parlor?**
   Grandmother
10. **Who killed the Trelors?**
    The handyman Ruben
11. **Where was the answer to the murders hidden?**
    Letter in the bookshelf
12. **What was the title of the book the letter was found in?**
    A Doll's House
13. **In what book does a play written by Henrik Ibsen solve the mystery and crime?**
    The Dollhouse Murders

## Final Battle: Culmination

All the teams from the classroom battles will gather to play for the title and, of course, the pizza party for their class.

Gather the participants at the library tables. Put team names on each table and once again hand out scrap paper and have the teams write down their team name.

This is a good time to remember PR. Invite the superintendent, principal, parents, and the local newspaper. If no reporter is available, write up your own article and email it to the editor. This is your chance to shine and shout about reading.

Videotape the contest and if technology in your school allows for it, send the video feed to the classrooms while the final battle happens, allowing the other sixth graders to watch the tournament. This format avoids restless audiences and still allows a full grade to be part of the action.

• PR – invite parents, school officials, and local newspapers
• Film the tournament with a video camera

A successful tradition will be set for success each year.

## Assessment

Excitement was built into reading and a common dialogue about 10 special books was created. One sixth grader was overheard saying, "We're going to kick your gluteus!" The students wanted to win the competition.

Circulation almost quadrupled in the midst of the program. There were long checkout lines in the library at the beginning of the school day.

**CIRCULATION STATISTICS**

**John Glenn Middle School Library – Total student enrollment, 534**

| Month | Check Outs 2003 | Check Outs 2004 | Increase with Battle of the Books/ Reading Playoffs |
|---|---|---|---|
| January | 286 | 440 | more than 50% |
| February | 233 | 787 | more than tripled |
| March | 238 | 925 | almost quadrupled |
| April | 317 | 652 | more than doubled |

| Month | Check Outs 2004 | Check Outs 2005 | Check Outs 2006 |
|---|---|---|---|
| January | 440 | 329 | 540 |
| February | 787 | 854 | 535 |
| March | 925 | 941 | 769 |
| April | 652 | 271 | 559 |

Figure 2.18: Circulation Statistics

# 𝕭𝖆𝖙𝖙𝖑𝖊 𝖔𝖋 𝖙𝖍𝖊 𝕭𝖔𝖔𝖐𝖘          **Your Opinion Counts**

In honor of next year's 𝕭𝖆𝖙𝖙𝖑𝖊 𝖔𝖋 𝖙𝖍𝖊 𝕭𝖔𝖔𝖐𝖘, give your honest opinion on the different activities and explain why (be specific). The Knighthood greatly values your thoughts.

| | |
|---|---|
| Did you like creating a team poster? Why? | |
| What contests did you like (e.g., bookmarks, crowns, or rap)? Why? | |
| Which books were "keepers?" Why? | |
| What books would you remove from the list? Why? | |
| What would you tell incoming sixth graders about Battle of the Books? | |
| What did you like about Battle of the Books? | |
| Did you think all members of your team did their part? Why or why not? | |
| Do you think there was enough time to read all the titles? | |
| What did you think of the competitions, classroom and final battle? | |

Figure 2.19: Evaluations

When students evaluated Battle of the Books they wrote:

"You're going to like the Battle of the Books because it makes reading fun and there's competition."

"I'd tell them it is a cool way to read, draw, and make creative things."

"It was fun, and don't get too nervous if you make it to the battle, [or] you forget all the answers."

"That it is awesome because you can win ice cream."

Cooperation, teamwork, and competition had worked its magic. Battle of the Books was destined to be part of the school culture. Teachers and students would own the program and look forward to participating each year. You have added an essential piece to the reading culture.

## Works Cited

Kelly, Joanne. *The Battle of the Books*. Englewood: Teacher Ideas Press, 1990.

# CHAPTER THREE

# *Reading Playoffs*

## *(A Tweaked Version of Battle of the Books)*

Seventh grade students were ready to do battle again. They remembered the enjoyment of working together on costumes, reading, and competition. Seventh grade teachers recognized the benefits of the program, but felt the pressure of time and learning created by high stakes testing. Teachers wanted to continue the program, but needed to cull down the time on Battle of the Books extras to allow for maximum classroom instruction. A re-tooled Battle of the Books was born – Reading Playoffs – with built-in accountability for students, but with fewer weekly activities and fanfare. After each book is read, the student takes a short quiz in the library. Extra points are gathered by creating posters or raps or dressing up as a character from the books. Students still look forward to the competition and the celebratory pizza party.

Once again, we met to collaborate to address issues. Friday's Book and Spirit Check had consumed too many classroom minutes. Teachers felt some students had not read and allowed other members of their team to do all the work, which can be a problem with group assignments. We still wanted to recapture the excitement, but to find a way to ensure that all students read a minimum number of titles and were more accountable to English teachers. A new strategy was born to continue to encourage reading. Teachers used Reading Playoffs as a book report grade for the quarter.

## Book Choices
***Fever 1793*** by Laurie Halse Anderson
   Laurie Halse Anderson gets Mattie's YA attitude perfectly as she takes us back to Philadelphia of 1793. As the adolescent reader begins to relate to Mattie's gripes with her mother and her duties at the coffee house, the reader comes to understand the public health menace was yellow fever.

***Tangerine*** by Edward Bloor
   Paul Fisher and his family move to Florida. There in Tangerine County, the family's secret is uncovered while the author opens the reader's eyes about many issues confronting schools around sports and how boys and girls are chosen for teams.

***Tears of a Tiger*** by Sharon M. Draper

Sharon Draper's novels deal with teenage angst. The author is a former high school teacher who takes on suicide, abuse, alcoholism, and depression in her books. Young adults are easily drawn into these teenage problems.

***Stormbreaker*** by Anthony Horowitz

Alex Rider begins his adventure as a 14-year-old James Bond in the first book of this popular fiction series. A definite page turner, and many readers will want to complete the entire series.

***No More Dead Dogs*** by Gordon Korman

Teenagers recognize their world of teachers, friends, sports, and dramatics. Korman writes with authenticity and humor about a very honest boy, Wallace Wallace, who trades his football jersey for theater production.

***Son of the Mob*** by Gordon Korman

Korman gets teenage humor just right. In the first chapter, Vince discovers the body of Jimmy the Rat in the trunk of his car, ruining his plans to romance a date on the beach. Teens are drawn into this lively story.

***Hidden Talents*** by David Lubar

David Lubar's first novel is full of surprises. Students sympathize with Martin who has ended up in the school of last resort, where he must deal with bullies and horrible teachers. He discovers special talents that he and his friends use to cope with this dreadful school.

***Touching Spirit Bear*** by Ben Mikaelsen

Ben Mikaelsen paints a portrait of Cole Matthews who must submit to "circle justice." Cole's struggle with anger has led him to violence against another student. Thanks to his parole officer, Cole begins a journey to forgive himself, his parents, and his community on an isolated island in the Pacific Northwest.

***Soldier's Heart*** by Gary Paulsen

This intense and fast-paced book tells the story of Charley Goddard who enlists in the Union Army during the Civil War. Charley learns about the horrors of war and the terrible price of honor. This novel is based on a true account of a soldier from Minnesota.

***Stargirl*** by Jerry Spinelli

Leo Borlock narrates this story of a young woman who is her very own person. Originally quite popular, Stargirl pays the price of her individuality. Teenagers will understand the pull between the need to belong and the desire to stand out. High school can be a tough place.

**Bonus Books**
***The Thief Lord*** by Cornelia Funke

Funke, in this narrative tale, tells the adventure of homeless teenagers in modern day Venice with just a slight touch of fantasy.

***Good Night, Mr. Tom*** by Michelle Magorian

This novel, set in England during WWII, tells the story of Willie Beech, who is sent to the country to stay with Mr. Tom, an elderly widower willing to share his home and heart. Willie has been abused physically and spiritually and returns to health with Mr. Tom. A surprising twist in the novel adds to the suspense.

***Airborn*** by Kenneth Oppel

Popular Canadian author Kenneth Oppel spins an adventure tale for young Matt Cruse, who comes of age on an airship while in search of fantastical creatures with a young passenger, Katie.

## The Big Event

Essential to the success of the program is, again, an assembly in the auditorium to rev up enthusiasm. Wear a sporting costume, display the books, and challenge students to read. Have Nerf balls ready to toss to students as they answer questions correctly. Again booktalk the list and distribute the handouts that have been duplicated on different colored paper:

- Parent Letter  < see Figure 3.1 >

- Program Description  < see Figure 3.2 >

- Bookmarks  < see Figure 3.3 >

Remind students of ice cream rewards and the ultimate prize of the pizza party. The excitement will build.

## The New Rules

If your seventh grade population is homogeneous, require groups to read three titles. This speaks to a new accountability for seventh grade.

- Reading Requirements
  If the grade is heterogeneous, require high achievers to read four books, and reluctant readers to read two books within six weeks. Always create balanced groups as is done in Battle of the Books. Create larger groups for weaker readers to level the playing field.

- Quizzes and Answer Key
  Upon completion of a book, the student takes a short quiz in the library, which is graded by the librarian and returned to the English teacher.

- Costuming
  Three weeks into Reading Playoffs, students dress up as a character from one of the books (e.g., Civil War soldier from Soldier's Heart).

- Extra Books
  High-powered readers are offered three challenge books.

## Motivational Projects

Students complete all of the following projects as part of their English grade.

# Reading Playoffs!

The seventh graders are now engaged in the playoffs!

Over the next six weeks, students will be involved in Reading Playoffs. This program is our seventh-grade version of Battle of the Books.

Teams of students commit to reading 10 books during that period. Enthusiasm is maintained through various contests (team posters, spirit outfits, and question contests). Students will take brief comprehensive quizzes on the books read.

After six weeks the teams will be asked questions about the books recalling specific details from each. One winning team from each English class will compete for first place. The top two winning teams will face off in a final playoff _____. The result will be a championship team from the seventh grade. The first place winning team will earn a pizza party for their class.

This communication is meant to enlist your support and ask that you encourage your child's reading efforts at home. Please sign the slip below and return it to your child's English teacher.

- - - - - - - - - - Tear Off - - - - - - - - - - - - - - - Return to School - - - - - - - - -

I acknowledge that my child _____

is participating in the Reading Playoffs.


Parent Signature_____Date_____

Figure 3.1: Parent Letter

Dear Seventh Grade Reading Players,

**The Charge!**

For the next six weeks, in teams you'll be reading 10 books, much like Battle of the Books. After completing a book, you'll take a short quiz in the library.

| Week 1 | • Return Parent Letter<br>• Create a team poster illustrating a sports theme |
|---|---|
| Vacation | Vacation Week – READ! |
| Week 2 | READ! |
| Week 3 | • Students dress up as character from one of the books. Each team should vary book titles. |
| Week 4 | READ! |
| Week 5 | Extra Point Grabbers (Projects)<br>• Create a bookmark<br>• Character sketch – personality chart with five adjectives<br>• Poem or rap of at least 10 lines<br>• Book advertisement for Amazon.com |
| Week 6 | Classroom Playoff:<br>Students dressed in spirit outfits compete to win. |
|  | Final Playoff:<br>Winner from each group competes in their spirit outfit for the grand prize of a class pizza party. |

There are some built-in extra challenges as well:
- 3 Bonus Books will offer teams an opportunity to earn extra points. When students create a poster, the poster must illustrate theme, plot or characterization

**The Playoffs**

At the Classroom Playoffs, students are to be seated by team. One or two questions will be asked for each book on the list. As a team, students decide the best answer for the question. The Team Captain writes the answer along with the author's last name on a piece of paper and gives the paper to the librarian. At that time, the extra points that the teams have earned are added to the score.

Winning teams will be selected from each of the seventh grade English classes as a result of the Classroom Playoffs. Those teams will compete in the Final Playoff to earn a pizza party for their entire class. Their names will be displayed in the library and announced over the PA system.

**Team Captain's Responsibility:** Keep track of the books read by his/her team members. The Team Captain also keeps track of the team's extra points. Every book on the list should be read by at least two team members. Students should memorize book titles and authors' last names in order to receive points during the Classroom and Final Playoffs. The Captain must also make sure that a team poster is submitted to the library.

And what about ice cream coupons? On Fridays, the principal will read questions and provide a ballot box. The first correct answer will earn those free ice creams.

May the best team win!

Figure 3.2: Program Description: The Charge

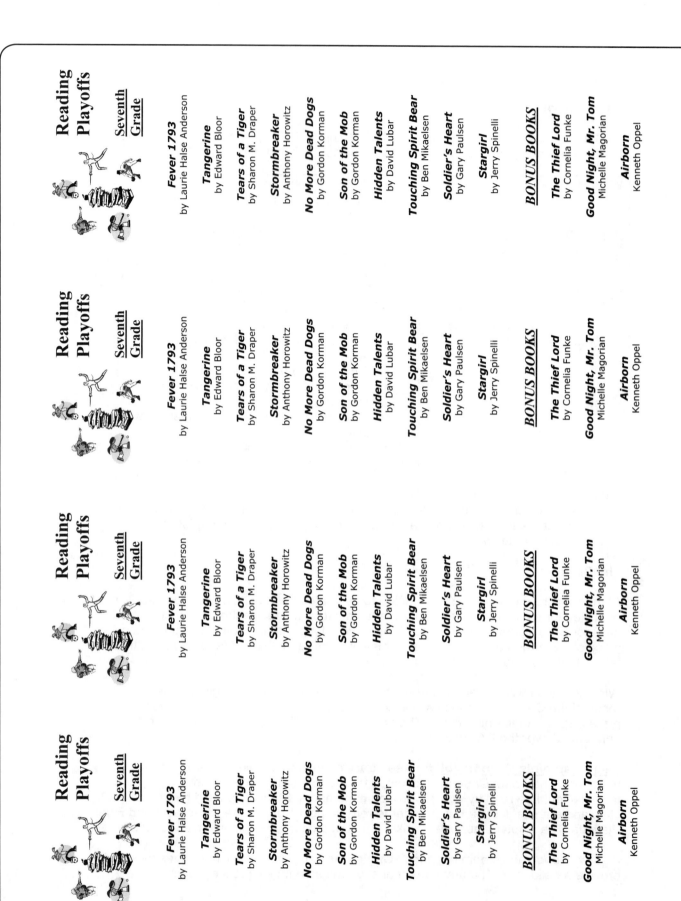

## Reading Playoffs

**Seventh Grade**

***Fever 1793***
by Laurie Halse Anderson

***Tangerine***
by Edward Bloor

***Tears of a Tiger***
by Sharon M. Draper

***Stormbreaker***
by Anthony Horowitz

***No More Dead Dogs***
by Gordon Korman

***Son of the Mob***
by Gordon Korman

***Hidden Talents***
by David Lubar

***Touching Spirit Bear***
by Ben Mikaelsen

***Soldier's Heart***
by Gary Paulsen

***Stargirl***
by Jerry Spinelli

**BONUS BOOKS**

***The Thief Lord***
by Cornelia Funke

***Good Night, Mr. Tom***
Michelle Magorian

***Airborn***
Kenneth Oppel

Reading Playoffs

Seventh Grade

Fever 1793
by Laurie Halse Anderson

Tangerine
by Edward Bloor

Tears of a Tiger
by Sharon M. Draper

Stormbreaker
by Anthony Horowitz

No More Dead Dogs
by Gordon Korman

Son of the Mob
by Gordon Korman

Hidden Talents
by David Lubar

Touching Spirit Bear
by Ben Mikaelsen

Soldier's Heart
by Gary Paulsen

Stargirl
by Jerry Spinelli

BONUS BOOKS

The Thief Lord
by Cornelia Funke

Good Night, Mr. Tom
Michelle Magorian

Airborn
Kenneth Oppel

Reading Playoffs

Seventh Grade

Fever 1793
by Laurie Halse Anderson

Tangerine
by Edward Bloor

Tears of a Tiger
by Sharon M. Draper

Stormbreaker
by Anthony Horowitz

No More Dead Dogs
by Gordon Korman

Son of the Mob
by Gordon Korman

Hidden Talents
by David Lubar

Touching Spirit Bear
by Ben Mikaelsen

Soldier's Heart
by Gary Paulsen

Stargirl
by Jerry Spinelli

BONUS BOOKS

The Thief Lord
by Cornelia Funke

Good Night, Mr. Tom
Michelle Magorian

Airborn
Kenneth Oppel

Reading Playoffs

Seventh Grade

Fever 1793
by Laurie Halse Anderson

Tangerine
by Edward Bloor

Tears of a Tiger
by Sharon M. Draper

Stormbreaker
by Anthony Horowitz

No More Dead Dogs
by Gordon Korman

Son of the Mob
by Gordon Korman

Hidden Talents
by David Lubar

Touching Spirit Bear
by Ben Mikaelsen

Soldier's Heart
by Gary Paulsen

Stargirl
by Jerry Spinelli

BONUS BOOKS

The Thief Lord
by Cornelia Funke

Good Night, Mr. Tom
Michelle Magorian

Airborn
Kenneth Oppel


Figure 3.3: Bookmarks

**Reading Playoffs**

**Seventh Grade**

Name_____
Team Name_____
Date_____

COUPON

**Reading Playoffs**

**Seventh Grade**

Name_____
Team Name_____
Date_____

COUPON

**Reading Playoffs**

**Seventh Grade**

Name_____
Team Name_____
Date_____

COUPON

**Reading Playoffs**

**Seventh Grade**

Name_____
Team Name_____
Date_____

COUPON

**Reading Playoffs**

**Seventh Grade**

Name_____
Team Name_____
Date_____

COUPON

**Reading Playoffs**

**Seventh Grade**

Name_____
Team Name_____
Date_____

COUPON

**Reading Playoffs**

**Seventh Grade**

Name_____
Team Name_____
Date_____

COUPON

**Reading Playoffs**

**Seventh Grade**

Name_____
Team Name_____
Date_____

COUPON

Figure 3.4: Ice Cream Coupons

# QUIZ: *Fever 1793*

**(Fill in the blank with the correct answer.)**

1) _____ lived two blocks away from Mattie's coffee house.

2) President Washington planned to go to _____ in September.

3) Dr. Kerr _____ Mattie's mother to cure her of yellow fever.

4) Grandfather instructed Mattie that a soldier needed _____, a full belly, and a decent night's sleep.

5) Mrs. Flagg thought the _____ doctors were better at saving yellow fever patients than the British doctors.

6) Volunteers from the _____ Society helped the nurses at Bush Hill.

7) After Mattie and her grandfather returned home, they both took _____ in the kitchen.

8) Mattie awoke to a morning _____, which would signal the end to yellow fever.

9) Mattie's mother returned in a wagon following _____.

10) Yellow fever was spread by _____.

Figure 3.5: QUIZ: *Fever 1793*

# QUIZ: Tangerine

## (Fill in the blank with the correct answer.)

1) Paul and his family moved to Tangerine County, Florida, from _____, Texas.

2) At Lake Windsor everybody makes the soccer team, but only (#)_____ Kids get to go to "away" games.

3) Coach Walski told Paul he couldn't be on the team because he would not be acceptable to the _____ company since he was visually handicapped.

4) Extreme rain caused the portables to slide into a _____.

5) Paul felt a miracle happened because he now could go to _____.

6) _____ was humiliated in the final play of Seagulls vs. Cypress Bay.

7) A volunteer firefighter says that _____ fires don't go out.

8) When Paul finally tells Tino he ratted him out at the carnival, Tino _____.

9) _____ became the county soccer champions.

10) Mr. Donnelly wrote that _____ was the greatest quarterback in the history of Tangerine County.

Figure 3.6: QUIZ: Tangerine

Name____________________ Class_____________ English Teacher____________________

# *QUIZ: Tears of a Tiger*

**(Fill in the blank with the correct answer.)**

1) _________________________________ blames himself for the death of Rob.

2) The judge took away Andy's driver's license until age _____________________.

3) Andy's mother dressed in high heels and silk dresses at ___________________.

4) The Hazelwood High School basketball team is known as the _______________.

5) Andy told Dr. Carrothers that he found a note on his locker that said __________________________________.

6) When Keisha and Andy went to the mall at Christmas time, Keisha sampled __________________________________.

7) A phone call from _________________________ depressed Andy at Christmas.

8) ________________ was talking to Andy in his dreams, which caused him to wake up screaming.

9) While discussing Shakespeare's ______________________________, Andy reacts to the lines, "Life's but a walking shadow."

10) After Andy's death, his parents _____________________________________________.

Figure 3.7: QUIZ: *Tears of a Tiger*

Name_____ Class_____ English Teacher_____

# QUIZ: *Stormbreaker*

## (Fill in the blank with the correct answer.)

1)  Alex Rider is _____ years old.

2)  _____ hadn't really died in a car accident. He had been shot.

3)  John Crawley was the personnel manager at _____.

4)  Stormbreakers are _____.

5)  Alex decides to help _____ because he doesn't want to leave Brookland.

6)  RV stands for _____ Point.

7)  Smithers equipped Alex with a small tube, a Nintendo Color Game Bag, and a _____.

8)  A _____ occupied Herod Sayle's fish tank.

9)  Sayle and Alex played a game of _____, a cue sport, that Alex won handily.

10) The aquarium burst because Alex put _____ on the rivets.

Figure 3.8: QUIZ: *Stormbreaker*

Name________________ Class____________ English Teacher________________

# *QUIZ: No More Dead Dogs*

**(Fill in the blank with the correct answer.)**

1) Wallace's dad had told him a lie about fighting in the ____________________ War.

2) Steve Cavanaugh was team captain of the football team and played the position of ______________________________.

3) In order to practice the flea-flicker, Wallace hooked the team into painting his ____________________.

4) Parker Zit was the nickname for ____________________, the newspaper reporter.

5) "If we don't mess it up, we make it up" was the motto of ____________________.

6) Rick Falconi thought Old Shep referred to a ____________________, not a dog.

7) Wallace noticed a shelf of pepper inside ____________________ locker.

8) Someone poured ____________________ on Mr. Fogelman's filing cabinet.

9) Rachel Turner always writes letters to ______________________________.

10) Mr. Fogelman played the ____________________ with the Dead Mangoes.

Figure 3.9: QUIZ: *No More Dead Dogs*

Name____________________ Class_____________ English Teacher___________________

# *QUIZ: Son of the Mob*

**(Fill in the blank with the correct answer.)**

1) Vince gets dating advice from his friend, ____________________________________.
2) Vince found ________________________________________ in the trunk of his car.
3) Vince found a diamond in his ____________________________________________.
4) Vince cannot play ____________________ because his father will not let him get hurt.
5) Tommy lives in an apartment in New York's __________________________.
6) Vince gets arrested on ______________________________________ charges.
7) Permethrin is the cure for ________________________________.
8) Vince visits Ray to buy a __________________________________.
9) ________________________________ created an internet betting operation.
10) ____________________ had to leave town because he was an undercover cop.

Figure 3.10: QUIZ: *Son of the Mob*

Name________________________ Class_______________ English Teacher______________________

# *QUIZ: Hidden Talents*

**(Fill in the blank with the correct answer.)**

1) __________________________________ is the name of the school Martin attends.

2) ______________________________________ gave Martin a tour of his new school.

3) Mr. __________________________ has muscles that looked like they were beginning to drip.

4) Kids play ______________________________________________________ at the library.

5) Martin was kicked out of _________________________ schools.

6) When _______________________________ knocks Frank off a ladder, he breaks his arm.

7) _______________________________________________________ was telepyric.

8) _______________________________ cards, also known as ESP cards, test psychic powers.

9) __________________________ had the power to make people angry and to strike and slash.

10) When Martin leaves for school, his father then picks on his _________________________.

Figure 3.11: QUIZ: *Hidden Talents*

# QUIZ: Touching Spirit Bear

### (Circle the correct answer.)

1) As the novel begins, Cole is
   a. beating up a classmate
   b. riding a skiff to an island
   c. robbing a store
   d. attending a Circle of Justice meeting

2) Cole beats up
   a. Peter
   b. Garvey
   c. his mother
   d. Edwin

3) What is devil's club?
   a. weapon
   b. shrub
   c. social organization
   d. rock group

4) Circle justice was meant to
   a. punish
   b. heal
   c. teach
   d. embarrass

5) Who suggests that Cole and Peter go to the pond alone?
   a. Edwin
   b. Garvey
   c. mother
   d. Spirit Bear

6) Cole, Edwin and Garvey spot a
   a. coyote
   b. wolf
   c. rainbow
   d. harbor seal

7) Cole was very satisfied when he
   a. rowed a boat
   b. built a shelter
   c. cooked bear
   d. chopped wood

8) The first animal Cole carves in the totem pole is a
   a. bear
   b. eagle
   c. beaver
   d. wolf

9) Cole made tree ornaments for Christmas out of
   a. wood
   b. pine cones
   c. aluminum foil
   d. feathers

10) Defiant describes
   a. Edwin
   b. Garvey
   c. Cole
   d. Peter

Figure 3.12: QUIZ: *Touching Spirit Bear*

Name____________________ Class_____________ English Teacher__________________

# *QUIZ: Soldier's Heart*

**(Fill in the blank with the correct answer.)**

1) Post-traumatic stress disorder is often a result of ____________________________.

2) In WWII the mental damage was called ________________________________.

3) During WWI the damage from war was called _____________________________.

4) Charley lived in Winona, ____________________________________________.

5) Charley had never traveled on a ______________________________________.

6) A surgeon told the soldiers to wear clean clothing in case ____________________.

7) At the battle of ______________________________, Massey died and two bullets collided in mid-air.

8) Bull Run was a creek that ran by ______________________________ Junction.

9) Charley traded coffee beans for __________________________ with a Rebel soldier.

10) The doctor told Charley to build a wall around the infirmary with _________________ to stop the wind.

Figure 3.13: QUIZ: *Soldier's Heart*

# QUIZ: *Stargirl*

### (Circle the correct answer.)

1) What did Leo get on his fourteenth birthday?
   a. a new car
   b. a huge party
   c. a porcupine necktie
   d. a tennis racket

2) What was Stargirl's real name?
   a. Sandy
   b. Crystal
   c. Cinnamon
   d. Susan

3) When it was someone's birthday, Stargirl liked to
   a. play her ukulele and sing "Happy Birthday" to him or her
   b. throw a huge party and invite all their friends
   c. paint a billboard sign with a Happy Birthday message
   d. send them an email birthday card

4) Why did people first start coming to see the Electrons play?
   a. to see Stargirl cheering and acting crazy on the ball field
   b. because the Electrons started winning
   c. because ticket prices were drastically reduced
   d. to see the players in their brand-new uniforms

5) Why did the students at Mica High School begin to hate Stargirl?
   a. because she started acting snobby when she became popular
   b. because she acted and dressed strangely
   c. because she cheered for the opposing team
   d. because they didn't like her rat

Figure 3.14: QUIZ: *Stargirl*

# QUIZ: Stargirl (continued)

**(Circle the correct answer.)**

6) What happened when Stargirl took to the Hot Seat?
    a. The student jurors attacked her with angry words.
    b. She became even more popular than before.
    c. Stargirl sang a song and the show was a hit.
    d. Stargirl became so shy that she couldn't speak.

7) Who did Stargirl fall in love with?
    a. Kevin
    b. Wayne
    c. Bobby
    d. Leo

8) After Stargirl and Leo were shunned by the students,
    a. Stargirl changed into Susan, a perfectly normal girl.
    b. Stargirl ran away from home and lived in the desert.
    c. Stargirl and Leo ran away and got married.
    d. Stargirl tried out for the basketball team.

9) Stargirl won the State _____ Contest.
    a. Spelling
    b. Oration
    c. Geography
    d. Writing

10) The last time anyone saw Stargirl was
    a. Leo's birthday party
    b. Graduation Day
    c. the night of the Ocotillo Ball
    d. the last basketball game

Figure 3.14: QUIZ: *Stargirl (continued)*

## Reading Playoffs
**Answer Key to Quizzes**

### Fever 1793
1. President Washington
2. Virginia
3. bled
4. boots
5. French
6. Free African
7. baths
8. frost
9. George Washington
10. mosquitoes

### Tangerine
1. Houston
2. 15
3. insurance
4. sinkhole
5. Tangerine Middle School
6. Erik
7. muck
8. kicks Paul
9. Tangerine War Eagles
10. Antoine Thomas

### Tears of a Tiger
1. Andy
2. 21
3. basketball games
4. Tigers
5. killer
6. perfumes
7. Rob's mother
8. Rob
9. Macbeth
10. separated or divorced

### Stormbreaker
1. 14
2. Ian Rider
3. Royal and General
4. computers
5. Alan Blunt
6. Rendezvous
7. yoyo
8. jellyfish or Portuguese Man-of-War
9. snooker
10. zit cream

### No More Dead Dogs
1. Vietnam
2. receiver
3. garage
4. Parker Schmidt
5. Bedford Weekly Standard
6. sheep
7. Feather's
8. pancake syrup
9. Julia Roberts
10. electronic keyboard

### Son of the Mob
1. Alex
2. Jimmy Rat
3. Cracker Jack box
4. football
5. Greenwich Village
6. auto theft
7. head lice
8. cell phone
9. Tommy
10. Ray

### Hidden Talents
1. Edgeview Alternative
2. Torchie
3. Acropolis
4. checkers
5. 3
6. Bloodbath
7. Torchie
8. Zenner
9. Martin
10. sister

### Touching Spirit Bear
1. B
2. A
3. B
4. B
5. B
6. B
7. B
8. B
9. C
10. C

### Soldier's Heart
1. war
2. battle fatigue
3. shell shock
4. Minnesota
5. steamboat
6. they were hit by a rifle ball
7. Bull Run (or Manassas)
8. Manassas
9. tobacco
10. dead bodies

### Stargirl
1. C
2. D
3. A
4. A
5. C
6. A
7. D
8. A
9. B
10. C

Figure 3.15: Reading Playoffs Answer Key to Quizzes

# Reading Playoffs

**Project Details**

Each student will do a different project each week. Ultimately, each student will have completed four different projects.

**Bookmark**

Standard bookmark size
Only one title per bookmark
Original artwork (Do not duplicate the cover of the book.)
On back of bookmark, your name and team name

**Character Sketch**

Hand drawn sketch in color in setting from the plot
8 ½ x 11
Example: Soldier in battlefield (*Soldier's Heart*) or Maddy in coffee house (*Fever 1793*)
5 descriptive adjectives

**Poem or Rap**

10 lines per person (e.g., a group rap would mean 3 people = 30 lines)
Expresses theme, action from the plot, or characterization (e.g., for *Tears of a Tiger*, rap about the car crash)

**Book Advertisement**

Like the ones on Amazon.com
4 to 8 lines
Blurb should contain at least one detail from the book.
Why would someone want to pick this book to read?

1. Character day
   - Students dress up as a character from one of the books.

2. Book ad
   - Create a book ad on a poster illustrating theme, plot, or characterization.

3. Poem or rap
   - Ten lines per person
   - Perform as a team
   - Express theme, plot, or characterization

*These additional projects can earn extra points for students to accrue prior to classroom battles.*

Figure 3.16: Reading Playoffs

**Weekly Incentives**

Excitement is generated through Friday book questions.

The principal asks questions on the spot in the cafeteria during lunchtime. Correct answers earn students free ice cream coupons.

## Friday Questions

**From *Touching Spirit Bear* by Ben Mikaelsen:**
For what sport did Cole try out in school? ***Wrestling***

**From *Tangerine* by Edward Bloor:**
What position does Paul play on the soccer team? ***Goalie***

**From *Tears of a Tiger* by Sharon Draper:**
Who believes Andy is a coward for his actions? ***Gerald***

**From *Stargirl* by Jerry Spinelli:**
What character stated that the hero was Gentlemen's Quarterly? ***Wayne Parr***

**From *Fever* 1793 by Laurie Halse Anderson:**
What are Grandfather's last words to Mattie? ***Love you***

**From *Hidden Talents* by David Lubar:**
Teri writes to her brother, Martin, and tells him she made a dinner. What was it? ***Lasagna***

Figure 3.17: Friday Questions

**Staple Rules**

- Teachers will select teams.
- Members create a team poster with a sports theme. A team captain is designated by the teacher.
- Students return the parent letter.
- The captain's responsibility is to record who has read which books.

**Culminating Playoffs**

Classroom playoffs produce the teams that will attend the final competition. After six weeks, a winning team will be crowned.

### Reading Playoffs
# Book Answer

Date_____

Name_____

Team Name_____

English Teacher_____

Answer_____
_____
_____
_____
_____

### Reading Playoffs
# Book Answer

Date_____

Name_____

Team Name_____

English Teacher_____

Answer_____
_____
_____
_____
_____

### Reading Playoffs
# Book Answer

Date_____

Name_____

Team Name_____

English Teacher_____

Answer_____
_____
_____
_____
_____

### Reading Playoffs
# Book Answer

Date_____

Name_____

Team Name_____

English Teacher_____

Answer_____
_____
_____
_____
_____

Figure 3.18: Friday Questions Answer Form

# Reading Playoffs

## Seventh Grade

Team Name_____English Teacher_____

Team Captain_____

Team Members_____

_____

_____

_____

_____

_____

| Author | Title | Assigned to |
|--------|-------|-------------|
| Anderson | *Fever 1793* | |
| Bloor | *Tangerine* | |
| Draper | *Tears of a Tiger* | |
| Horowitz | *Stormbreaker* | |
| Korman | *No More Dead Dogs* | |
| Korman | *Son of the Mob* | |
| Lubar | *Hidden Talents* | |
| Mikaelsen | *Touching Spirit Bear* | |
| Paulsen | *Soldier's Heart* | |
| Spinelli | *Stargirl* | |

Points_____

## BONUS BOOKS

| Author | Title | Assigned to |
|--------|-------|-------------|
| Funke | *The Thief Lord* | |
| Magorian | *Good Night, Mr. Tom* | |
| Oppel | *Airborn* | |

Points_____

Figure 3.19: Team Assignment Form

**Group Name** _____

**LG** _____

| Team Members | Fever 1793 | Tangerine | Tears of a Tiger | Stormbreaker | No More Dead Dogs | Son of the Mob | Hidden Talents | Touching Spirit Bear | Soldier's Heart | Stargirl | **\*\*BONUS\*\*** | |
|---|---|---|---|---|---|---|---|---|---|---|---|---|
| | | | | | | | | | | | | |
| | | | | | | | | | | | | |
| | | | | | | | | | | | | |
| | | | | | | | | | | | | |

- ■ Fill in entire box when a book is finished.
- ◨ Fill in half a box if a book is in progress.

Figure 3.20: Team Record Keeper

# Questions & Answers for Classroom & Final Playoffs
### *Fever 1793* by Laurie Halse Anderson

1. **In what war had Grandfather fought?**
   American Revolution

2. **From what did Polly die?**
   Yellow fever

3. **What was the name of Grandfather's green parrot?**
   King George

4. **Who invited Mattie and her mother to tea?**
   Mrs. Ogilvie

5. **What did Mattie use to try and catch fish?**
   Petticoat

6. **Where did the authorities at Bush Hill want to send Mattie?**
   Orphan house

7. **Where were the people who died from yellow fever buried?**
   Potter's Field

8. **What did Mattie force the gravediggers to do at her grandfather's burial?**
   Pray

9. **Where did Eliza and Mattie bring the sick children?**
   Coffee house

10. **Who does Mattie ask to be her partner in the coffee house?**
    Eliza

11. **How did Mattie's father earn a living?**
    Carpenter

# Questions & Answers for Classroom & Final Playoffs

### *Tangerine* by Edward Bloor

1. **What type of fish is stocked in the lake where the Fishers live?**
   Koi

2. **What do Paul and his mother note about the sports fields their tour of Lake Windsor Middle School?**

   Fields are flooded

3. **What was the nickname Erik and Arthur had for Mike Costello?**
   Mohawk Man

4. **Who coached the War Eagles soccer team?**
   Betty Bright

5. **Who hit Luis with a blackjack?**
   Arthur

6. **How did Mike Costello die?**
   Struck by lightning

7. **Why was Paul expelled?**
   Assaulted a teacher

8. **To what city were Grandpop and Grandmom on their way?**
   Orlando

9. **Of whom has Paul always been afraid?**
   Erik

10. **What did Paul need blue pants, white shirts, and blue ties to do?**
    Attend St. Anthony's

11. **Who actually sprayed paint into Paul's eyes when he was a child?**
    Vincent Castro

## *Questions & Answers for Classroom & Final Playoffs*

### *Tears of a Tiger* by Sharon Draper

1. **Who is Andy's girlfriend?**
   Keisha

2. **Why is it that B. J. did not make the Hazelwood High basketball team?**
   Too short

3. **What kind of problem did Gerald's father have?**
   Drinking

4. **What position did Rob play on the basketball team?**
   Center

5. **What gift did Keisha give Andy for Christmas?**
   Sweater

6. **Who was the first person to talk about death with Andy?**
   Dr. Carrothers

7. **Which teacher called Andy's parents to report about his grades?**
   Ms. Blackwell, English teacher

8. **Who drew a picture of a tiger with tears?**
   Monty

9. **When Andy makes a desperate call to Dr. Carrothers, what is he told?**
   He is out of town.

10. **With what weapon does Andy kill himself?**
    Gun

## Questions & Answers for Classroom & Final Playoffs

### *Stormbreaker* by Anthony Horowitz

1. **From what country had Jack Starbright come?**
   America

2. **What was the name of the auto wreckers?**
   J. B. Stryker/Stryker and Sons

3. **In what city did Sayle grow up?**
   Cairo

4. **Even though the other agents called him "Double O Nothing," what was Alex's actual training name?**
   Cub

5. **Who did Mrs. Jones tell Alex had killed Ian Rider?**
   Yassen Gregorovich

6. **Where did Mr. Grin work before he was employed by Sayle?**
   Circus

7. **By what means did Yassen arrive on the carnival beach?**
   Submarine

8. **Who releases Alex from his handcuffs?**
   Nadia Vole

9. **Who shoots the Prime Minister?**
   Alex

10. **At the conclusion of Stormbreaker, who kills Sayle?**
    Yassen

11. **How did Alex arrive at the science museum?**
    Parachute

## *Questions & Answers for Classroom & Final Playoffs*

### *No More Dead Dogs* by Gordon Korman

1. **What is the best policy for Wallace?**
   Honesty

2. **Who is Wallace's ex-best friend?**
   Steve Cavanaugh

3. **What did Wallace have to serve on the first day of play rehearsal?**
   Detention

4. **Who went to the library to read Teen Dazzle magazine?**
   Trudi

5. **What was in the bucket that fell on the cast of performers?**
   Pepper

6. **Who rode a moped during the play?**
   Lazlo

7. **Who felt like Benedict Omelette?**
   Wallace

8. **What was "The Void's" real name?**
   Myron

9. **Who was the author of the play, "Old Shep, My Pal"?**
   Zack Paris

10. **Who provided the soundtrack for the play?**
    Dead Mangoes

11. **Who was pictured in the poster in Wallace's room?**
    George Washington

12. **Who planted a cherry bomb on the stuffed dog?**
    Dylan

# Questions & Answers for Classroom & Final Playoffs

### *Son of the Mob* by Gordon Korman

1.  **In what type of business does the Luca family pretend to be, in case the FBI is listening?**
    Vending machine business

2.  **Name the Web site that Alex created for his new media class.**
    www.misterferraridriver.com

3.  **What is the nickname that the Luca family has for Kendra's father (the FBI agent)?**
    Agent Bite Me

4.  **Vince catches something from Kendra. What does he catch?**
    Lice

5.  **What does Vince ask Ray for, so that he can make plans with Kendra?**
    A cell phone (stolen)

6.  **Who does Vince try to help when he can't pay Mr. Luca money that he owes him?**
    Jimmy the Rat or Ed Mishkin

7.  **Who did Vince send in his place to meet Kendra's father?**
    Alex

8.  **What is the name of the coffee shop that Ed Mishkin opened with help from Jimmy the Rat?**
    Java Grotto

9.  **What is the name of the tape that Vince has of Kendra singing?**
    K-Bytes

10. **What type of car does Vince drive?**
    Mazda

11. **Who put signs up at school to vote for Vince and Kendra for Homecoming?**
    Alex

12. **What was the internet site, iluvmycat.usa, that Vince made being used for?**
    Horse race betting

13. **What supposedly happened to Ed and Jimmy the Rat's bar, The Platinum Coast, so that they could collect insurance money?**
    Hit by lightning

14. **Who does Vince believe is an FBI insider in his father's business?**
    Ray Francione

15. **Who gave the order for the Calabrese murder?**
    Vince's mother, Mrs. Luca

# Questions & Answers for Classroom & Final Playoffs

### *Hidden Talents* by David Lubar

1. **Name the school Martin attends in Hidden Talents.**
   Edgeview Alternative School

2. **From how many schools had Martin been expelled?**
   3

3. **Who gave Martin a tour of his new school?**
   Torchie

4. **At his first meal in Edgeview, Martin thought he was eating potatoes, but they were actually what vegetable?**
   Turnips

5. **What board game do the kids at Edgeview play in the library?**
   Checkers

6. **To what teacher did Martin say, "I'm not bald."**
   Mr. Parsons

7. **Who had muscles that looked like they were beginning to drip?**
   Mr. Acropolis

8. **Marin had to act like what character from history in Ms. Crenshaw's class?**
   Thomas Jefferson

9. **What did the kids from town call the students from Edgeview?**
   Alters

10. **Which friend of Martin was telepyric?**
    Torchie

11. **What word means the power of the group to achieve an effect greater than they can achieve as individuals?**
    Synergy

12. **What happens to Flinch when Bloodbath knocks him off the ladder?**
    He breaks an arm.

13. **Who had the power to make people angry, to strike, and to slash?**
    Martin

14. **When Martin finally punches Bloodbath, of whom is Martin reminded?**
    His Father

## Questions & Answers for Classroom & Final Playoffs

### *Touching Spirit Bear* by Ben Mikaelsen

1. **What is the full name of the main character in Touching Spirit Bear?**
   Cole Matthews

2. **What crime did the main character commit against Peter Driscal?**
   He assaulted Peter, smashing his head against the surface of a parking lot.

3. **What is "Circle Justice"?**
   A system based on Native-American traditions that attempts to provide healing for the criminal offender, the victim, and the community

4. **Why does the main character consent to "Circle Justice"?**
   He would go to prison otherwise.

5. **To what drug is the main character's mother addicted?**
   Alcohol

6. **The main character is banished to a remote island off the coast of which state?**
   Alaska

7. **The "Spirit Bear" appears principally in the legends of which ethnic or racial group?**
   Native American Indian

8. **What is the name of the main character's Native-American parole officer?**
   Garvey

9. **What kind of creature attacks and seriously injures the main character?**
   A bear

10. **What color is the "Spirit Bear"?**
    White

11. **Eventually the main character starts a large carving project. What is he carving?**
    A totem

12. **By what means does the main character try to escape his island?**
    Swimming

13. **The main character is an abusing person, but he is also a victim of abuse. Who is his principal physical abuser?**
    His father

14. **The main character in the story shows many signs of hating himself, but there is another character in the novel who attempts suicide. Who is that?**
    Peter Driscal

15. **What does the term "devil's club" mean?**
    A spiny shrub of western North America

# Questions & Answers for Classroom & Final Playoffs

### *Soldier's Heart* by Gary Paulsen

1. **How much money did Charley get paid in the Army?**
   $11.00

2. **Name the fort that Charley enlisted at to fight for the Civil War.**
   Fort Snelling

3. **In what state did Charley see his first African American?**
   Maryland

4. **What did Charley think lanterns were at night?**
   Fireflies

5. **What wound caused the new soldier, Nelson, to die?**
   Stomach wound

6. **What meat was served to the sick soldiers?**
   Horse meat

7. **To whom did Charley send his money earned as a soldier?**
   Mother

8. **At what battle was Charley wounded?**
   Gettysburg

9. **According to Gary Paulsen, at what age did the real Charley die?**
   23

10. **Charley received coffee beans from a Southern soldier after he had given him what item?**
    Tobacco

11. **How old was Charley when he enlisted in the Army?**
    15

# Questions & Answers for Classroom & Final Playoffs

*Stargirl* by Jerry Spinelli

1. **In what state does *Stargirl* take place?**
   Arizona

2. **What is the name of the story's narrator?**
   Leo Borlock

3. **What was the first present *Stargirl* gave Leo?**
   A necktie with porcupines on it

4. **What is the name of the high school?**
   Mica Area High School

5. **What is the name of the in-school TV show?**
   Hot Seat

6. **What instrument did *Stargirl* play?**
   Ukelele

7. **What was the job of the jury on the in-school TV show?**
   To ask the guest questions that would make the guest uncomfortable

8. **Who is Cinnamon?**
   Stargirl's rat

9. **What was the name of the group that met at Archie's?**
   Loyal Order of the Stone Bone

10. **What did *Stargirl* want Leo to do when they got to her special "enchanted" place in the desert?**
    Nothing or as close to nothing as they can get

11. **What does shunning mean?**
    Not speaking to and ignoring someone

12. **In what type of contest was *Stargirl* participating?**
    Oratorical contest

13. **What video did *Stargirl* want to rent when she was at the mall with Leo?**
    "When Harry Met Sally"

14. **What does *Stargirl* do when she is happy?**
    She puts a pebble in a wagon.

15. **What did the sign say that *Stargirl* painted for Leo?**
    "Stargirl loves Leo"

16. **What was the name of the basketball player who broke his ankle from the other high school?**
    Kovac

17. **What was *Stargirl's* real name – her full name?**
    Susan Julia Caraway

18. **What is the name of the dance *Stargirl* led at the Ocotillo Ball?**
    The bunny hop

19. **How did *Stargirl* respond when Hillari slapped her?**
    Stargirl kissed her on the cheek.

20. **What is the name of the high school club that promises to do one nice thing a day for someone else?**
    Sunflowers

**Reading Playoffs**                    **Your Opinion Counts**

In honor of next year's Reading Playoffs, give your honest opinion on the different activities and explain why (be specific). The Playoffs Committee greatly values your thoughts.

| | |
|---|---|
| What did you like about creating a team poster? | |
| Which projects did you like (e.g., bookmarks, raps, advertisement)? | |
| Which character did you choose to develop a costume? | |
| How did Reading Playoffs compare to Battle of the Books in sixth grade? | |
| Which books were "keepers?" | |
| What books would you remove from the list? | |
| What would you tell incoming seventh graders about Reading Playoffs? | |
| Did you think all members of your team did their part? | |
| Do you think it would be fair to evaluate who really did read books for credit, not just honor? | |
| What did you like about Reading Playoffs? | |

Figure 3.31: Evaluation

## Assessment

Even though evaluations showed some found "the tests really annoying," others enjoyed getting "goofy when dressed up." Some students were happy there were no book reports, and others enjoyed listening to the created "raps." The most significant factor is that all were reading as evidenced by our circulation statistics.

An additional benefit of both programs is the common dialogue created around books. When future teachers make reference to historical fiction, many students will have read *Soldier's Heart* or *The Watsons Go to Birmingham – 1963*. If teachers want to discuss characterization, students can recall Cole Matthews or Joey Pigza. If the discussion is about mysteries, Dovey Coe may come to mind. Sharing the conversation about books will help students sustain their future love of story because students have shared their opinions and experiences about books with their peers and have experienced the satisfaction of completing multiple titles, many for the first time. The book list has appealed to reluctant readers and has satisfied the students who quickly ask, "Can I get out another book?"

**CIRCULATION STATISTICS**

**John Glenn Middle School Library – Total student enrollment, 534**

| Month | Check Outs 2003 | Check Outs 2004 | Increase with Battle of the Books/ Reading Playoffs |
|---|---|---|---|
| January | 286 | 440 | more than 50% |
| February | 233 | 787 | more than tripled |
| March | 238 | 925 | almost quadrupled |
| April | 317 | 652 | more than doubled |

| Month | Check Outs 2004 | Check Outs 2005 | Check Outs 2006 |
|---|---|---|---|
| January | 440 | 329 | 540 |
| February | 787 | 854 | 535 |
| March | 925 | 941 | 769 |
| April | 652 | 271 | 559 |

Figure 3.32: Circulation Statistics

**CHAPTER FOUR**

# *Booked Conversation*

With what do you follow the success of Battle of the Books and Reading Playoffs? What can you offer eighth graders to energize their reading?

Booked Conversation is designed to acknowledge the increasing maturity of eighth graders and to tap into a new way of discussing books. Instead of teamwork and competition, Booked Conversation elevates the book culture to a higher level, thereby building student self-confidence. Instead of classmates talking with each other about books as in Battle of the Books and Reading Playoffs, with this program the conversation is a one-on-one with a faculty member. Teachers get involved in a personal way with students around books. Here books become a tool for interaction with adults.

Students earn coupons by arranging to meet with a teacher after they have read a sponsored book from the list that is posted prominently in the library. If a student gathers three coupons, he or she gets invited to a pizza party near the end of the school year. The returned coupons enter the student into drawings for prizes. Students take on the responsibility of arranging the meeting or conversation at a time that works for both teacher and student. Obtaining a coupon from the library, the student requests the teacher to sign the coupon attesting to the fact that the book has been read. Provide teachers with a list of discussion points to help them determine if the student has read the book. Try to get as many eighth-grade teachers involved as possible. Eighth graders usually prefer to meet with their current teachers rather than their instructors from sixth or seventh grade. Also allow teachers to add some of their favorite titles to the list. They will really enjoy discussing them with students.

In order to have success with Booked Conversation, once again collaborate with English and reading teachers to develop a book list that provides both easy and challenging reads. Teachers who want students to read more academically demanding books will be satisfied, and the needs of more reluctant readers will be met by including easy reads, the kind of books that immediately grab the reader. Ultimately you will create a compelling book list for eighth graders.

Near the end of middle school, eighth graders are often totally self-absorbed and act as if they know it all. Many start to physically resemble high schoolers, but may still be middle schoolers emotionally. This duplicitous creature presents a thorny task to the librarian who wants to pick just the right title for these young teens. The differences in this age group can be significant. Teenagers at this age may be avid readers ready for adult titles. However, librarians still need to tread carefully around provocative and incendiary issues in novels even as they move the students forward to more mature titles. Some students may be reading adult books like *The Da Vinci Code* by Dan Brown and Sue Monk Kidd's *The Secret Life of Bees*, while others will be content to read YA titles that reflect their life in high school like Laurie Halse Anderson's *Twisted* or Terry Trueman's *Stuck in Neutral*.

## Book Choices

Six of the titles are compelling science fiction/fantasy novels. **Skybreaker** by Kenneth Oppel is an adventure/fantasy that continues the adventures of Matt Cruse, who came of age on an airship in **Airborn**. Nancy Farmer's **The House of the Scorpion**, set in the land somewhere between California and Mexico, takes a hard look at cloning. **Ender's Game** by Orson Scott Card describes how Ender Wiggin, Child-Warrior, battles against the "buggers." **Double Helix** is a modern thriller by Nancy Werlin, which looks at genetic engineering from a young man's point of view. In Neal Shusterman's **The Dark Side of Nowhere**, Jason must figure out just what it means to be human after he discovers he is an alien living on Earth. Andrew Clements, in his novel **Things Not Seen**, makes his main character invisible. Before Bobby becomes visible, the reader will have shared quite a compelling adventure with him.

Two books tell the stories of people caught up in war. Adam Bagdasarian, in his fictionalized biography **Forgotten Fire**, retells the horrors of the Armenian holocaust. **In My Hands**, an autobiography by Irene Gut Opdyke, recounts the heroism of one young woman who saved the lives of her Jewish friends by hiding them in the house of the German general for whom she worked.

Robert Cormier's **The Chocolate War** and William Golding's **Lord of the Flies** are both classics that examine evil and its effects on our society.

Mark Haddon's **The Curious Incident of the Dog in the Night-Time**, an adult bestseller, is a mystery told from the point of view of a boy with autism.

Two classics are included in the list. **To Kill a Mockingbird** by Harper Lee continues to mesmerize readers with its tale spun in the American South, and **Of Mice and Men** by John Steinbeck captures the story of migrant workers.

Two biographies provide compelling stories. Jeannette Walls' memoir, **The Glass Castle**, an Alex Award winner, will mesmerize the reader with the author's story of growing up as part of a dysfunctional family in the midst of mind-boggling poverty. Jack Gantos' biography, **Hole in My Life**, tells the popular author's story of how selling drugs during his high school years landed him in jail.

**A Northern Light** by Jennifer Donnelly is historical fiction set in the Adirondacks at the turn of the century. A young heroine, Mattie Gorkey, has a tough life on a farm with her widowed father and younger siblings. This story will not only enlighten young women about women's issues, but also will involve them in Mattie's tough choice for her future. **Montmorency: Thief, Liar, Gentleman?** by Eleanor Updale is historical fiction set in nineteenth- century London. Montmorency leads a double life as gentleman by day and thief by night.

Many teenagers tend to like contemporary stories with which they can identify and relate. Often they disdain science fiction and fantasy. They want to recognize real issues in a teenager's life.

Male readers particularly respond to fiction by Walter Dean Myers. **Monster** offers up a tale of Steve Harmon who is on trial for murder. Using a book with a varied format, Myers examines moral issues while the reader awaits the results of the case.

Students will be amazed at the adventure of Pi Patel crossing the ocean in a lifeboat with a 450-pound Bengal tiger in **Life of Pi** by Yann Martel.

In **Prom** Laurie Halse Anderson's main character, Ashley, rises to the occasion to save the senior prom. Finding the perfect voice for Ashley, the author transforms an ordinary high school kid into a reluctant, contemporary heroine.

In Joan Bauer's **Rules of the Road**, teenager Jenna Boller takes her job of selling footwear at Gladstone Shoes so seriously, her employer pays her to drive her to Texas in her Cadillac. The book is filled with humor, and girls relate to Jenna's spunky and responsible spirit.

In **Forged by Fire**, the second book in Sharon Draper's popular Hazelwood High Trilogy, Gerald, one of the basketball players from **Tears of a Tiger**, confronts sexual abuse of his half-sister.

**The Secret Life of Bees** by Sue Monk Kidd tells the powerful story of 14-year-old Lilly, who runs away from her abusive father. She takes Rosaleen, a black woman who cared for her, along as well. Rosaleen had been beaten and jailed by bigots. Both find comfort and rebirth with three black women who are beekeepers.

Patricia McCormick takes on teenage issues. In **Cut**, Callie's story comes to life as she deals with her problem of cutting. The reader listens to the pained voice of the main character as she sorts through her problems in a therapeutic residential facility.

Sonya Sones in **What My Mother Doesn't Know** provides us with great chick-lit. Our heroine, Sophie, speaks in free verse, but shares so much teenage angst that female readers will not stop reading until the final page.

Jordan Sonnenblick's **Notes from the Midnight Driver** opens with a car crash, but fortunately in this YA novel no one dies. However, Alex does get sentenced to hours of community service with a cantankerous old man, Sol Lewis. The two eventually connect through music, and readers will be quite satisfied with the culminating concert at the nursing home.

**I Am the Wallpaper** by Mark Peter Hughes showcases Floey Parker, who tires of never being noticed. When her spiteful cousins post pages from her diary on the Internet, Floey gets even.

In **Make Lemonade**, Virginia Euwer Wolff brings 14-year-old LaVaughn to life as she babysits for a single 17-year-old mom with two children.

**Stuck in Neutral**, Terry Trueman's first novel, is a story of 14-year-old Shawn, who suffers from cerebral palsy. Everyone assumes he is a human vegetable, but the author creates a character who is intelligent and totally aware but who cannot communicate his knowledge with friends and family. The cliffhanger is that Shawn suspects his father's plans to euthanize him.

John Feinstein uses basketball's Final Four as a backdrop in his mystery, **Last Shot: A Final Four Mystery**. Two eighth graders, after winning a journalism writing contest, uncover a blackmail scheme to fix a game.

**Silent to the Bone** by E. L. Konigsburg is a tried and true suspense novel. Who injured Branwell's baby sister? The author slowly uncovers the guilty party through silent conversations between Branwell and his friend, Connor.

When eighth-grade English teachers reserve the library for book selection, seize the opportunity to introduce Booked Conversation. Explain the program and tell the eighth graders about potential prizes and the final party. Booktalk the titles on the list to generate enthusiasm. Be clear that students will need to read three books from the faculty sponsored list to be part of the culminating pizza prize party. Allow the program to run for two quarters to provide the needed time to read at least three books and meet with teachers.

At a faculty conference in June before summer break or early in the year, recruit teachers to sponsor books. English and reading teachers will be easy to convince, but attempt to get guidance counselors and other subject teachers involved. I remember a special moment one year when two girls discussed Ruth White's **Memories of Summer** with the male gym teacher. That was a conversation that would never have happened without this program.

Meanwhile set about gathering prizes for the party, which is a PR opportunity. In this way, people in the community learn about valuable programs you organize in your library. When you request donations, you will be explaining how many books students will be reading. The community will gain a positive impression of the school library. Local merchants will be happy to donate small prizes when asked. Rewards from the local video store or bookstore are ideal. Be sure to write thank you notes and keep a file of names and phone numbers for successive years. As part of an article for the school newsletter and local newspaper, recognize the merchants for their contributions, providing them with public acknowledgment for their generosity.

## Timetable

- Collaborate with teachers to create the book list.

- Call for sponsors at a faculty conference or via email.

- Hand out program description to eighth graders in English classes.

- Publish the sponsored book list and have it available at the library.

- Create coupon and invitation.

- Begin trolling for prizes.

- Establish a celebration date and invite the students who have read at least three books.

- Recognize community donors.

- Assess student opinions about books read.

This program illustrates that all of the faculty, not only the English department, thinks reading is important. In addition, it is also a clever way to introduce young adult literature to teachers who may only remember *Treasure Island* and *Red Badge of Courage*, the books they read as teenagers. YA books can be a revelation to teachers who have never been exposed to the best in children's literature.

The opportunity to talk about books with individual teachers validates students' opinions and supports literary conversation. Students will be ready for a more sophisticated high school model. After all, they've participated in book conversation for three years.

# Booked Conversation
# Eighth Grade

 Book List

| Author | Title |
|--------|-------|
| Anderson, Laurie Halse | *Prom* |
| Bagdasarian, Adam | *Forgotten Fire* |
| Bauer, Joan | *Rules of the Road* |
| Card, Orson Scott | *Ender's Game* |
| Clements, Andrew | *Things Not Seen* |
| Cormier, Robert | *The Chocolate War* |
| Donnelly, Jennifer | *A Northern Light* |
| Draper, Sharon | *Forged by Fire* |
| Farmer, Nancy | *The House of the Scorpion* |
| Feinstein, John | *Last Shot: a Final Four Mystery* |
| Gantos, Jack | *Hole in My Life (BIO)* |
| Golding, William | *Lord of the Flies* |
| Haddon, Mark | *Curious Incident of the Dog in the Night-Time* |
| Hughes, Mark Peter | *I Am the Wallpaper* |
| Kidd, Sue Monk | *Secret Life of Bees* |
| Konigsburg, E. L. | *Silent to the Bone* |
| Korman, Gordon | *Son of the Mob* |
| Lee, Harper | *To Kill a Mockingbird* |
| Martel, Yann | *Life of Pi* |
| McCormick, Patricia | *Cut* |
| Myers, Walter Dean | *Monster* |
| Opdyke, Irene Gut | *In My Hands: Memories of a Holocaust Rescuer (BIO)* |
| Oppel, Kenneth | *Skybreaker* |
| Shusterman, Neal | *The Dark Side of Nowhere* |
| Sones, Sonya | *What My Mother Doesn't Know* |
| Sonnenblick, Jordan | *Notes from the Midnight Driver* |
| Spinelli, Jerry | *Stargirl* |
| Steinbeck, John | *Of Mice and Men* |
| Trueman, Terry | *Stuck in Neutral* |
| Updale, Eleanor | *Montmorency: Thief, Liar, Gentleman?* |
| Walls, Jeannette | *The Glass Castle* |
| Werlin, Nancy | *Double Helix* |
| Wolff, Virginia Euwer | *Make Lemonade* |

Figure 4.1: Booklist

# Booked Conversation

# Call for Sponsors

**Booked Conversation** is a reading motivation program for eighth graders. Basically kids earn coupons for doing outside reading. **Booked Conversation** adds the staff interaction piece that prepares students for the high school summer reading format.

Students select books from a large list of titles that will be sponsored by members of the faculty. Students return signed coupons to the library. At the end of the quarter, students with three or more coupons enjoy a pizza party at which the coupons are used to draw for prizes.

Some books are challenging and others are easy reads. Books may have multiple sponsors.

After a student has read one of the books on the list, he or she will make an appointment with the sponsoring teacher to discuss the book. The student will obtain a coupon from the library which you are to sign if you feel the student has read the book and can give you their feelings about the book. The library will keep track of the number of books read by each student.

Listed below are some **questions** you may wish to ask to help students to reflect on the books they have read:

- How did you respond to this book?

- What was the ending of this book? How did that make you feel?

- Tell me about the characters. Which ones did you like and dislike?

- What do you think the author was trying to say?

Figure 4.2: Call for Sponsors

# Eighth Grade
# Booked Conversation

For the next six weeks, you will have an opportunity to win prizes at a pizza party.

All you need to do is read three books that are sponsored by one of the teachers. Check at the circulation desk for the names of the book sponsors.

It works like this:

- ❑  You read the book from the list.
- ❑  Get a blank coupon.
- ❑  Make an appointment with the sponsoring teacher.
- ❑  Talk about the book one-on-one with the teacher.
- ❑  Have the teacher sign the coupon.
- ❑  Return it to the library.

Students who have three signed coupons will be invited to the party featuring prizes.

Figure 4.3: Program Description

# Booked Conversation

Name_____

English Teacher_____

Book Title_____

Author_____

Sponsor's Signature_____

Discussion Date_____Hour_____

*Return coupon to _____.*

# Booked Conversation

Name_____

English Teacher_____

Book Title_____

Author_____

Sponsor's Signature_____

Discussion Date_____Hour_____

*Return coupon to _____.*

# Booked Conversation

Name_____

English Teacher_____

Book Title_____

Author_____

Sponsor's Signature_____

Discussion Date_____Hour_____

*Return coupon to _____.*

# Booked Conversation

Name_____

English Teacher_____

Book Title_____

Author_____

Sponsor's Signature_____

Discussion Date_____Hour_____

*Return coupon to _____.*

Figure 4.4: Coupon

## Invitation to

*Booked Conversation*

## Pizza & Prizes
## Party

## Invitation to

*Booked Conversation*

## Pizza & Prizes
## Party

## Invitation to

*Booked Conversation*

## Pizza & Prizes
## Party

## Invitation to

*Booked Conversation*

## Pizza & Prizes
## Party

Figure 4.5a: Party Invitations

_____
(student name)

# You are cordially invited to attend the

*Booked Conversation*

## Pizza & Prizes Party!

Time:
Place:

_____
(student name)

# You are cordially invited to attend the

*Booked Conversation*

## Pizza & Prizes Party!

Time:
Place:

_____
(student name)

# You are cordially invited to attend the

*Booked Conversation*

## Pizza & Prizes Party!

Time:
Place:

_____
(student name)

# You are cordially invited to attend the

*Booked Conversation*

## Pizza & Prizes Party!

Time:
Place:

Figure 4.5b: Party Invitations

**School Library**
**Street Address**
**City, State  Zip Code**

Booked Conversation

Date

Community Donor
Store Name
Street Address
City, State  Zip Code

Dear _____,

    Thank you so much for the donation to our **Booked Conversation** reward event. Eighth graders who read three or more books in a six-week period and discussed these books with faculty members are coming together to celebrate at a pizza party and participate in free drawings.

The school and our community of parents really appreciate your support.

                         Yours truly,

                         Teacher/Librarian

Cc:    School Superintendent
       Principal

Figure 4.6: Donor Thank You

Name_____

Assessment Sheet
# Booked Conversation

Sometimes books can create totally different responses for different people.

Title_____

Author_____

| What did I think about this book? | What did the teacher think about this book? |
|---|---|
|  |  |

How do these responses compare?

Figure 4.7: Assessment

**CHAPTER FIVE**

# Author Visits

Author visits are special. They promote literacy. Often for the first time students get to meet a living, breathing author, dispelling the notion that all authors are dead like Shakespeare. Author visits provide students with an opportunity to learn how authors craft their work and write for young adults. Students may never have considered writing as an actual profession, but authors often tell their listeners about the fun of writing novels in their pajamas and getting paid too! An author visit presents an opportunity for students to converse directly with an established author. Students will be inspired and reenergized. When seventh graders saw the library set up for Jack Gantos' annual visit with the sixth grade, they showed enthusiasm. Jack, that venerable composer of story, had mesmerized and entertained them the previous year when they were in sixth grade. Now they eagerly asked him endless questions while he readied his materials at the podium for incoming classes. His visit had been an extraordinary event.

Preparing for an author visit says "special moment." You will need to work for the success of this event to ensure that the memory will remain both powerful and lasting. Once again, librarians and teachers need to work together to ensure a successful visit. Familiarizing the students with the author and his body of work is the scaffold of a memorable visit. Working with classroom teachers, the librarian achieves a "wow" moment. Students will become enthused as they prepare for a well-known author whose work is familiar. Utilize a checklist to organize the events.

## *Author Checklist*

### Planning

- ☐ Search for authors
- ☐ Meet with teachers
- ☐ Select readings for kids
- ☐ Accumulate biographical information
- ☐ Schedule the event on the school calendar
- ☐ Choose a presentation date

### Teaching

- ☐ Research lesson
- ☐ Literature lesson

### Publicity

- ☐ Parent letter
- ☐ School newsletter
- ☐ Alert school administration
- ☐ Contact local newspaper

### Arrangements

- ☐ Hotel room
- ☐ Check

### Performance day

- ☐ Room set-up
- ☐ Digital camera
- ☐ Video camera
- ☐ AV/computer needs
- ☐ Lunch plans

### Follow-up

- ☐ Thank you's
  - ○ Author
  - ○ Hotel GM
  - ○ Parents
- ☐ Student assessment

Figure 5.1: Author Checklist

## Search and Find

Locate an outstanding author who is a good presenter for middle school. A great author may not be a performer for middle school. Before inviting an author, try to attend a workshop or convention where you can hear him or her speak. Use your local library organizations' listserv to get feedback and suggestions on whom to invite. Other librarians will be useful to contact for advice. Many authors have Web sites, which offer ease of communication. Authors may utilize publisher reps to schedule their visits.

Our school has hosted Jack Gantos, Graham Salisbury, and Yoko Kawashima Watkins for sixth grade. Gordon Korman, Stephanie Spinner, Ben Mikaelsen, David Lubar, and Liza Ketchum have spoken to our seventh graders. Sharon Draper was chosen for our eighth graders. The key to success is careful preparation with students.

Inviting local authors eliminates travel expenses. You might cost share with other schools to host an out-of-town author. Three schools in our area shared expenses to welcome Ben Mikaelsen. We divided up his travel expenses and arranged his transportation among schools and the airport. Sometimes local grants will fund the cost of an author visit, or parent organizations may raise money for the event. Funds from magazine drives, school dances, or enrichment budgets can be utilized. Even funds from book fairs can be utilized for a special event.

## Student Preparation

### Read Works

Students were eager to meet David Lubar. His first book, **Hidden Talents**, is popular and one of the selections for Reading Playoffs. David is a prolific short story writer and his stories are easily located in various collections. Teachers can help students become familiar with David's short but provocative short stories so that students will be prepared with questions and comments. David encourages students to email him and he will respond.

Gordon Korman's story, "A Reasonable Sum," a truly funny story, is available for reproduction from his Web site: <*www.gordonkorman.com*>. All of the seventh graders read it. **Son of the Mob** and **No More Dead Dogs** are popular selections on the Reading Playoffs list. Students met the author in the intimate library setting.

Ben Mikaelsen's **Touching Spirit Bear** is also a title available on Reading Playoffs. Ben is an excellent presenter and his life story of living with a 700-pound bear and adventures with airplanes and boats grabs the listener. Familiarity with the author and his work is vital to success.

Liza Ketchum was very effective with seventh graders. Her book, **Orphan Journey Home**, was originally serialized in the *Boston Herald* in 1999. English teachers prepared the students by having their classes read sections of the story as it had been divided in the newspaper. Groups retold the story. In one day, everyone was familiar with the story and the students had practice summarizing and retelling the story.

Information literacy skills were addressed in the library. Students used databases, advanced Google, and the author's Web site to research data about Liza and her books and to prepare to have a meaningful dialogue.

Name_____     Class/Teacher_____

Ben Mikaelsen, a well-known young adult book author, will be presenting at our school. Many of us are familiar with his book, *Touching Spirit Bear*. To learn some facts and information about the author, use the following library resources and answer the numbered questions.

## Library Resources

| Search information | Questions | Answers |
|---|---|---|
| Go to **Galenet Student Resource Center**<br>Search with the words: Touching Spirit Bear<br>Select the article from *The Book Report* | According to the book review, what does the white spirit bear do to Cole Matthews? | |
| Go to **Infotrac**<br>Use **Biography Resource Center**<br>At Name Search: Select<br>⊙ start of last name<br>Type in: Mikaelsen, Ben<br>Enlarge photo | Describe Ben Mikaelsen. | |
| Select the article from ***Authors and Artists for Young Adults*** | Where was Ben born?<br><br>Where does Ben live now?<br><br>What kind of adventures does he have? | |
| Go to **Infotrac**<br>Use **General Reference Center Gold**<br>Search with the words: Touching Spirit Bear<br>Select the article from *School Library Journal* (February 2004) | As a result of circle justice, where will Cole be sent?<br><br>What does Cole learn about his anger? | |
| Go to the **Web site**<br>www.benmikaelsen.com | How many books has Ben written?<br><br>What can you learn about Buffy? How long does he hibernate? How much does Buffy eat?<br><br>How long does it take to write a book? | |
| Now create **two** good questions of your own to ask Ben Mikaelsen on January 31st. | | |

Figure 5.2a/5.2b: Mikaelsen Prep Questions

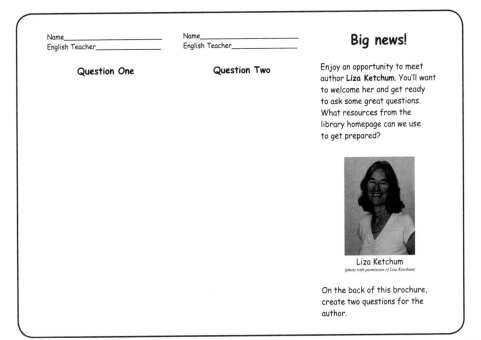

Name_____
English Teacher_____

Name_____
English Teacher_____

**Question One**

**Question Two**

**Big news!**

Enjoy an opportunity to meet author **Liza Ketchum**. You'll want to welcome her and get ready to ask some great questions. What resources from the library homepage can we use to get prepared?

Liza Ketchum
*(photo with permission of Liza Ketchum)*

On the back of this brochure, create two questions for the author.

Figure 5.3: Ketchum Brochure

Use **Biography Resource Center** to get information.

Find a magazine article on *Orphan Journey Home*.

In whose voice is the story told?

Where is it set?

How do the parents die?

Use **Advanced Search - Google**.

Use terms "milk sickness" and cows.

What caused milk sickness?

Visit Liza's Web site:

www.lizaketchum.com

Describe Liza's childhood.

How did Liza learn to write?

What are some of Liza's passions?

What awards has she received?

Figure 5.3b: Ketchum Brochure

Liza exhibited her galleys and discussed the editor's role in the process of revising and rewriting prior to publication. She answered questions from the eager audience about her life and work and her favorite novels.

After brainstorming the essentials of conflict, at Liza's direction, seventh graders composed and shared their own works of fiction. Student stories were crammed with fantasy and possibility and many were so enthused that they continued to compose at home.

Yoko Watkins' visit is always special. Sixth graders read her autobiographical novel **So Far from the Bamboo Grove** and look forward to meeting the author. They ask her about her life and the members of her family who escaped Japan at the end of WWII. The visit is very personal for both Yoko and her young readers. Students write letters to her before her presentation and enthusiastically ask her for her autograph. Teachers encourage students to write to her after they have heard her personal story.

## Author WebQuests

By integrating the research process around visiting authors, you can teach users about databases and Web sites to gather information. Students learned that David Lubar used to develop computer games, Sharon Draper was awarded "Teacher of the Year," Jack Gantos taught writing at Emerson College, and Gordon Korman disciplines himself to write every day.

At the end of each WebQuest, students gathered information about an author and learned to navigate Web sites and databases. They formulated questions to have ready on the day of the author visit. Develop the WebQuest in a brochure format. Use this opportunity to discuss what would be unacceptable questions such as, "How much money do you earn?" and so forth.

Name_____
English Teacher_____

Name_____
English Teacher_____

### News Flash!

**Question One**

**Question Two**

Enjoy an opportunity to meet author **David Lubar**. You'll want to welcome him and get ready to ask some great questions. What resources from the library homepage can we use to get prepared?

David Lubar & friend
*(photo with permission of David Lubar)*

On the back of this brochure, create two questions for the author.

Figure 5.4a: Lubar Brochure

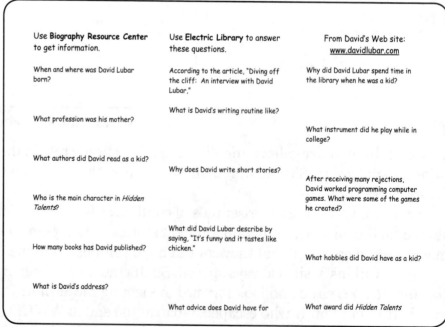

| Use **Biography Resource Center** to get information. | Use **Electric Library** to answer these questions. | From David's Web site: www.davidlubar.com |
|---|---|---|
| When and where was David Lubar born? | According to the article, "Diving off the cliff: An interview with David Lubar," | Why did David Lubar spend time in the library when he was a kid? |
| | What is David's writing routine like? | |
| What profession was his mother? | | What instrument did he play while in college? |
| What authors did David read as a kid? | | |
| | Why does David write short stories? | |
| | | After receiving many rejections, David worked programming computer games. What were some of the games he created? |
| Who is the main character in *Hidden Talents?* | | |
| | What did David Lubar describe by saying, "It's funny and it tastes like chicken." | |
| How many books has David published? | | What hobbies did David have as a kid? |
| What is David's address? | | |
| | What advice does David have for | What award did *Hidden Talents* |

Figure 5.4b: Lubar Brochure

Name_____          Learning Group_____

Sharon Draper, author of the Hazelwood High trilogy, will present at our school. Many of us have read her book, *Tears of a Tiger*. To learn some facts and information about the author, use the following library resources and answer the numbered questions.

## Library Resources

Go to **Galenet Student Resource Center**
     Search with the words: Sharon Draper
     Select the article from *Writing*

1) What is Sharon Draper's primary goal as a writer?

_____
_____
_____
_____

2) As Sharon Draper writes, how does she feel about her characters?

_____
_____
_____
_____
_____
_____

     Select the article from *Jet*

3) What is the name of the term paper that students write at Walnut Hills HS?

_____
_____
_____

Figure 5.5a: Draper Prep Questions

Go to **Infotrax**

      Use **Biography Resource Center**

      Select the article from ***Authors and Artists for Young Adults***

4) At what times in the day does Sharon Draper write her books?

_____

_____

_____

      Use **General Reference Center**

      Search with the words:  Tears of a Tiger

      Select the article from ***Publishers Weekly***

5) According to the review, what effect does the "MTV" approach create in the novel?

_____

_____

_____

Go to the **Web site** http://sharondraper.com/index.asp

      Follow Quick Links to ***Doing a report for school?***

6) What influences did Sharon's parents and childhood memories have upon her?

_____

Now create **two** good questions of your own to ask the author when you meet her in person.

1) _____

2) _____

Figure 5.5b: Draper Prep Questions

## Organize the Day

As the key organizer, your first job is to set up a workable schedule. Contact all the teachers who are involved in the day's activity to make necessary schedule changes. Authors frequently will do three presentations per day, and you will need to group the students with teachers.

As host, carefully introduce the author to the audience, taking the opportunity to remind students about proper behavior.

Many authors assume they'll be signing books. You might order copies of the author's books to have them for sale. Authors enjoy signing their books for students. Make time for that if it is part of the plan.

Attend to any media needs – overheads, screens, microphones, etc.

Make lunch preparations. Invite teachers, administrators, and parents to join the author for lunch. Purchase lunch for the author and have the others brown bag it.

## PR Opportunities

Be sure to have a digital camera on hand. At the very least, you can make a poster for the library and display it for all to see.

Invite the local newspaper to cover the event. Write your own article and email it to the editor along with your digital photos. Don't forget the school newspaper and photos for the yearbook.

Of course, invite parents via the school newsletter as well as the superintendent and principal. Write up the event for the PTO newsletter.

Suggest student reporters cover the event for the school newspaper.

## Follow Up

Try to arrange payment on the day of the visit. This is a perfect conclusion to a successful event.

Young readers can be encouraged to write to or email authors. Some authors like David Lubar encourage the students to email him. Yoko Watkins enjoys receiving handwritten mail and personally answers the students. Sharon Draper often reads heartbreaking stories from her correspondence with fans. Visiting schools is a financial plus for authors, but it is also a way to create a lasting impression with young readers.

## Additional Resources

Bulion, Leslie. "Make It Happen: Awesome Author and Illustrator Visits!" *Education World* (2001). 1 Dec. 2006 *<http://www.educationworld.com/a_curr/curr374.shtml>*.

Follos, Allison. "Making an Author's Visit Your Best 'Good Time.'" Teacher Librarian 31.5 (2004): 8-12. Expanded Academic ASAP. Thomson Gale. 1 Dec. 2006 *<http://find.galegroup.com>*.

Gutman, Dan. "The Perfect Author Visit." *Dan Gutman Children's Book Author.* 2004. 26 Feb. 2007 *<http://www.dangutman.compages/planvisits.html>*.

Ruurs, Margriet. "Optimizing Author Visits: Having a Children's Book Writer or Illustrator Can Be a Powerful Motivating Experience for Your Students—If You Follow Some Common-Sense Guidelines from a Writer Who's Been There." *Reading Today* 22.5: 20-22. *Expanded Academic ASAP*. Thomson Gale. 1 Dec. 2006 <http://infotrac.galegroup.com>.

**CHAPTER SIX**

# *Using Technology to Reel in Readers*

After viewing a presentation on video booktalks, an enthusiastic seventh grader stated, "I know what booktalk I want to do, but not what book." She had viewed her fellow seventh graders doing video booktalks and knew that she wanted to perform. Video Booktalk Kiosk couples the art of booktalking with the fun of technology.

In an article for *Library Media Connection* (October 2006, p. 56-59), Terence W. Cavanaugh outlined the concept of capturing a prepared student booktalk with a digital camera. When a student enters the library to select books, at a search station he or she clicks on a book cover image which reveals a classmate reciting a lively booktalk. Students easily accept another's recommendation. Once a student pronounces that a book is "really good," the searching customer is satisfied. In this way, student book endorsements are recorded for the entire school population. The project sets the stage for the video camera to capture student planned and rehearsed sales pitches of titles for fellow classmates.

The kiosk for this project is a standalone computer with a screen displaying book cover images. Selecting one will entertain the searching patron with a one-minute booktalk recommending a specific title.

Librarians, as professional booktalkers, can model how to perform booktalks and prepare students to create their own. We know that effective booktalks dramatically pique interest in available books and subsequently increase circulation.

Team up with language arts teachers to showcase this project. Teachers may be willing to give students extra credit if a student completes the video booktalk. This project is a marriage of language arts and technology.

## Instruction

Discuss what a booktalk really is. Make certain that students know it is not a summary or book review, but an advertisement or commercial for a book.

Model booktalks in a PowerPoint. I classified booktalks into five styles and modeled each one.

- **Read Aloud Passage**

  This works for books that have compelling passages. Such a title is ***Climb or Die*** (Myers, Edward. New York: Hyperion Books for Children, 996). Read the section where the protagonists are falling off the mountain.

- **Plot Synopsis**

  This style is particularly effective with mysteries. By sketching out the plot, the booktalker draws the listener into the intrigue. Roy Eberhardt's task to save the owl habitat in ***Hoot*** (Hiaasen, Carl. New York: Knopf, 2002) will engage listeners who will root for his victory over the Pancake House.

- **Introduce a Prop**

  Including a prop such as a hat, pen, or letter will spark interest. Using an old broom, talk about Mother Bloodwort in ***Which Witch?*** (Ibbotson, Eva. New York: Dutton Children's Books, 1999). Who put skunk grease on her broom?

- **Heartfelt Appeal**

  With this approach, students consider a problem and try to relate. It is especially effective with "problem" novels as the reader relates to the issues. When talking about ***My Brother's Keeper*** (McCormick, Patricia. New York: Hyperion Books for Children, 2004), ask students to decide if, ike Toby, they would keep a relative's drug abuse a secret.

- **Mood Accent**

  This style of booktalk utilizes dramatic appeal. Here is an opportunity to star in your own production. Using ***Dave at Night*** (Levine, Gail Carson. New York: HarperCollins, 1999), coax out a Yiddish accent and imitate old man Solomon Gruber or moan like Dave when he's pretending to be a medium at the Harlem Renaissance parties they attended.

Cavanaugh (p. 57) lists video booktalking sites. Have students view them and evaluate their effectiveness. Choose sites where students are doing the booktalking. Students will enjoy watching their peers. Provide an evaluation checklist.

Name_____ Class_____

# *Booktalking Critique*

1. **What type of booktalk is it?**
   - ❑ Read Aloud
   - ❑ Plot Synopsis
   - ❑ Introduce a Prop
   - ❑ Heartfelt Appeal
   - ❑ Mood Accent

2. **What was included that made it effective (content and delivery)?**

   _____

   _____

3. **What made it ineffective?**

   - ❑ Voice   _____
   - ❑ Gesture  _____
   - ❑ Content  _____
   - ❑ Prop    _____

4. **Based on the booktalk, why will other students want to read this book?**

5. **Based on the booktalk, why wouldn't you be interested in reading this book?**

Figure 6.1: Booktalking Critique

## Planning

Whatever free choice book the student selects, he or she can find a matching booktalk style.

Students script out their short one-minute booktalk and decide if they want to use a prop. A boy used a globe when discussing *Around the World in Eighty Days* by Jules Verne. A girl held up a pen and letter when booktalking *P.S. Longer Letter Later* by Paula Danziger and Ann Martin.

Students practice at home either memorizing the talk or writing organized notes to prompt them when in front of the camera.

## Rehearsal and Performance

Before filming, select a quiet spot with good light. Have students run through their lines and prepare for taping. Use a digital video camera that has the capability for files to be uploaded by cable into a computer, such as a Canon ZR800, which captures sound. Laptops offer the flexibility of holding large files and can be transported easily to classrooms. Take a photo of the book cover with a digital camera to attach to the video file. Upload the files into Moviemaker, which is free production software that can be used with Microsoft Windows XP (www.microsoft.com/moviemaker). Students will remain calm if you reassure them that if they're not satisfied, they can refilm.

## Evaluation

Students will have an opportunity to reflect on the effectiveness of their booktalks by using a self evaluation checklist. Students who see their classmates creating video booktalks are often inspired to produce their own.

A local cable station might be convinced to televise the final product. Consent forms for underage students will be necessary and should be available from the television access company.

When students spark conversation about books from a different vantage point, technology has an impact that continues to motivate middle school readers.

Teacher Name_____ Student Name_____ Reviewer Name_____

# Project: Video Booktalk Kiosk

**CATEGORY        RESPONSIBILITIES**

*Content*
- ❏ I used a strong attention-getting device.
- ❏ I used words that the audience could understand.
- ❏ My vocabulary was strong and unambiguous.
- ❏ I used facts and logical appeals where appropriate.
- ❏ I used opinions or emotional appeals where appropriate.
- ❏ I used supportive details.

*Delivery*
- ❏ My body language was alert and relaxed.
- ❏ My voice varied in pitch. It was not monotone.
- ❏ I used meaningful gestures.
- ❏ I used notes sparingly. I did not read from them unless presenting a quote.
- ❏ I didn't hesitate or lose my place.
- ❏ I didn't use filler words (e.g., um, uh, ah, like, mm).
- ❏ I didn't call attention to my errors by apologizing.
- ❏ I didn't fidget, rock back and forth, or pace.
- ❏ I maintained eye contact most of the time.
- ❏ My pronunciation was clear and easy to understand.
- ❏ My rate of speech was neither too fast nor too slow.
- ❏ My volume was neither too loud nor too soft.

*Presentation Aids*
- ❏ Presentation aids were used during the speech.
- ❏ Presentation aids were relevant to the topic.
- ❏ Presentation aids enhanced the speech or helped people remember the main points.

Worksheet created using toolkit from:
Project Based Learning. <pblchecklist.4teachers.org>. *Project Based Learning*. ALTEC, University of Kansas. 25 Sept. 2007 <http://pblchecklist.4teachers.org>.

Figure 6.2: Self Evaluation

Motivating Readers in the Middle Grades
Chapter Six: Using Technology to Reel in Readers
103

## Works Cited

Anderson, Sheila, *and Kristine Mahood.* "The Inner Game of Booktalking." *VOYA* Jun. 2001: 107-109.

Cavanaugh, Terence W. "Creating a Video Booktalk Kiosk." *Library Media Connection* Oct. 2006: 56-59.

Eaton, Gale. "How to Do a Book Talk." <www.maschoolibraries.org>. 9 Nov. 2006. MSLMA. 16 May 2007. <www.uri.edu/artsci/lsc/Faculty/geaton/MSLMAtalk/index.htm>.

PART
**TWO**

# Recommended Collection for Middle School

The pleading voice on the telephone asks if she can please bring her five language arts classes to the library to get books for this quarter's book report assignment. After checking the daily schedule, you acquiesce and graciously give the okay. Immediately you begin scurrying around the shelves to collect the books needed for this assignment. As the school librarian, you must pick titles at a moment's notice that students will enjoy and yet will satisfy the teacher's demand. So much for teacher/library collaboration!

Frequently real life school service really means instant service and expert knowledge of your book collection. This instantaneous demand for service will require the librarian to showcase and discuss perhaps 75 books at a moment's notice, and be ready for the challenge of finding books for each child who only wants science fiction, or sad books, or funny books, or skinny books, or who just plain hates to read.

Even after booktalks and offering suggestions, no doubt there will be a bewildered student who will ask, "Do you have any good books?"

My favorite reply is usually, "No, I only buy bad ones." Although some might roll their eyes, we can relax a little after I ask a few probing questions and suggest some possibilities. Much practice and knowledge will guide me around the bookshelves. I rely on the book titles I know that readers tell me are terrific. I often hand a student a book and tell them that no one ever complains about this one!

This portion of the book is meant to be a useful resource for librarians and teachers who want to know what to suggest for middle school students who are at the transition stage from elementary to high school. Your client may be happy reading a Betsy Byars' title or ready to take on **Lord of the Flies** by William Golding. Frequently reading level may have nothing to do with interest level. A student may be capable of reading Hemingway's **The Old Man and the Sea,** but not adult enough to be interested. **Stuck in Neutral** may require too much maturity from the reader even though it is just skinny enough for a reluctant one.

This guide focuses on middle school titles for the teacher/librarian who must suggest books that will both entertain and challenge the school population. Students at this age are not ready for the emotional angst that permeates young adult books. Sometimes described as "grit-lit," these themes are too adult for middle school. Descriptions of sex, drugs, alcohol, abuse, and sexual identity are too graphic and explicit. Students are maturing, but not quite ready to move beyond children's literature. Finding the right book for this group, frequently described as "tweens," to continue to motivate them to read for pleasure, is a daunting task. Your bag of tricks should include some titles that will encourage reluctant readers and others that will satisfy the insatiable ones. The books must cover the wide span of interest and reading levels that exist in middle school. When a student enters the library and wants to know if you have any good books, you will be ready to match the patron with the right title with confidence.

Students may ask if you've read every book in the library. I tell them, "Of course!" My recommended list is based on 30 years of experience as a librarian and teacher. Books selected for inclusion are worthy titles that are pleasurable to read. I've tried not to repeat titles already profiled in Part One. If reading is an enjoyable experience, we will build lifelong lovers of books and reading.

## Criteria for Selection

- Books received good reviews in professional journals.
- Many titles received awards or appeared on best books lists.
- Titles are popular with students.
- Books are highly readable because they tell a good story.
- Books offer meaningful reading and most are page turners.

## Additional Resources

Honnold, Rosemary. *The Teen Reader's Advisor*. New York: Neal-Schuman Publishers, Inc., 2006.

Jones, Patrick, et al. *A Core Collection for Young Adults*. New York: Neal-Shuman Publishers, Inc., 2003.

Lewis, Valerie V., and Walter M. Mayes. *Valerie & Walter's Best Books for Children: A Lively Opinionated Guide*. New York: HarperCollins Publishers, 2004.

Odean, Kathleen. *Great Books about Things Kids Love*. New York: Ballantine Books, 2001.

Odean, Kathleen. *Great Books for Boys*. New York: Ballantine Books, 1998.

Odean, Kathleen. *Great Books for Girls*. New York: Ballantine Books, 1997.

Rochman, Hazel. *Against Borders*. Chicago: ALA/Booklist Publications, 1993.

Silvey, Anita. *100 Best Books for Children*. Boston: Houghton Mifflin Company, 2004.

Silvey, Anita. *500 Great Books for Teens*. Boston: Houghton Mifflin Company, 2006.

# Adventure Books

Adventure books are crammed with thrills and chills. They take the reader on a journey down the Yukon or across the Atlantic or up a mountain or sometimes to other worlds. Adventure books are grounded in danger and excitement. Main characters face physical and mental obstacles that drive the plot and hook the reader on what will happen next. These books have special appeal to reluctant readers who crave page turners. Events carry the plot to a riveting outcome.

Of the following titles, some are tried and true while some are new players:

**Avi.** *The True Confessions of Charlotte Doyle*. New York: Avon Books, 1992.

Newbery Award winner Avi does not disappoint with this swashbuckling tale of a young girl crossing the Atlantic on a ship with 13 sailors. From the very beginning of the journey, Avi foreshadows the dark voyage that lies ahead. When the old black cook gives Charlotte a dirk to place under her pillow, the reader is immediately drawn into the story.

Girls will love the spunk of Charlotte, who becomes an able sailor. She is the fine young lady who rises to the occasion to sail the seas. This is an enjoyable tale for boys as well, as the action is nonstop. Avi keeps it up to the end and just when the reader is certain of the conclusion, there is a marvelous twist at the end. Grades 6-7

**Campbell, Eric.** *The Place of Lions.* San Diego: Harcourt Brace & Company, 1991.
For Chris and his father, Africa was to be a new beginning, but a plane crash in the Serengeti derails those plans. Dad and the pilot are both injured, and it is up to Chris to get some help. All alone, he realizes that no one knows the plane has crashed and he must make his way to access help. His odyssey is mirrored by a struggle in a nearby pride where the senior lion must defend his position. Campbell's prose is beautifully written as he takes on animal rights issues when Chris spots poachers. Ultimately, is Chris a hero? This 1990 novel is still an appealing title to have in a collection. Grades 7-8

**Hobbs, Will.** *Jason's Gold.* New York: Morrow Junior Books, 1999.  The year is 1897. When news of the discovery of gold in Canada's Yukon reaches 15-year-old Jason, he embarks on a 5,000 mile journey to strike it rich. Moose, bears, and a 500-mile trip down the Yukon River are just a few dangers Jason faces while he searches for his brothers. Hobbs writes from his own childhood experiences of growing up in Alaska: backpacking, canoeing, and rafting.

Readers will be caught up in the drama built upon the events of the Klondike Gold Rush, including historical figures such as Jack London. Grades 6-8

**Horowitz, Anthony. *Stormbreaker*.** New York: Scholastic, 2000.

Anthony Horowitz has created a series around a 14-year-old, Alex Rider, who takes over his uncle's job at the British intelligence agency, MI 6, after his questionable demise. Certainly Alex would make James Bond jealous as his escapades take him through London foiling all the bad guys. In this title, Alex must save the world from a dastardly plot involving kids and computers.

Readers who like action are immediately drawn into this book, and they will not be disappointed. There are several more books in the series. Grades 7-8

**Ibbotson, Eva. *Journey to the River Sea*.** New York: Puffin, 2003.

Give this one to the girls who like to read traditional adventure books with complicated plots. They will be drawn into the story of orphaned Maia and her governess, Miss Minton, who travel to Brazil to live with the dreadful Carter family, and try to serve hot English tea in the jungle. Grades 6-8

**London, Jack. *The Call of the Wild*.** New York: Scholastic, 1963.

This classic still calls to readers who want to stretch their reading vocabulary. Readers who respond to Will Hobbs will enjoy Buck's story. During the journey to the Yukon, a kidnapped dog becomes the leader of a wolf pack. This novel is set during the Gold Rush of 1896 with sled dogs, wolves, and survival of the fittest.

Animal lovers find this compelling narrative of the unforgettable hero, Buck, hard to put down. This is a crossover to historical fiction. Grades 6-8

**Mikaelsen, Ben. *Touching Spirit Bear*.** New York: Harper Collins, 2000. Mikaelsen combines adventure and contemporary issues in this nonstop novel. Cole Matthews has an attitude and is pretty savvy at playing the adults in his life, but when confronted with his banishment to an island in the North Pacific, he even challenges a large white spirit bear, only to be mauled. The scene where the seagulls begin to feed on his lacerated body will stay with readers for a long time.

Mikaelsen does not find an easy way for Cole to seek redemption, nor does he grow preachy about Cole's battle with the wilderness and his own soul. Grades 7-8

**Naylor, Janet Reynolds. *The Fear Place*.** New York: Aladdin Paperbacks, 1996.

Children who have siblings know anger felt with family members. Doug's feelings for his brother, Gordon, churn visibly in the opening chapter of this book. Doug must overcome his fear of heights in order to find his brother and, at the same time, survive impending danger of an attack by a stalking cougar.

Short and intense, this book will especially appeal to boys. Readers will be happy to know Naylor has written over 100 books. Grade 6

**Oppel, Kenneth. *Airborn*.** New York: EOS, 2004.

Students who love old-fashioned adventure will be taken in by Matt Cruse aboard a luxury airship, Aurora. When Matt saves an elderly balloonist, he learns that there are beautiful creatures inhabiting the skies. Then Matt meets young Kate de Vries, the balloonist's granddaughter, and together they battle pirates and discover cloud cats in a rollicking fantasy/adventure.

The male/female hero partnership makes this popular with both boys and girls. Grades 6-8

**Temple, Frances. *Grab Hands and Run*.** New York: Orchard Books, 1993.

Ask students if they even know where El Salvador is and if they could imagine getting to Canada on foot. This compelling page turner follows a refugee family as they plan to walk from Central America to Canada. Both girls and boys will respond to this suspenseful story about crossing the border. Grades 6-7

**White, Robb. *Deathwatch*.** New York: Bantam Doubleday Dell Books for Young Readers, 1972.

Older readers will respond to this classic good guy/bad guy story. A young fellow with good intentions and honor agrees to take a bad guy hunting. Ben follows the rules, but Maddox does not. When he accidentally shoots an old fellow and refuses to call police, the story get tense as Maddox takes Ben's clothes, gun, supplies and, more importantly, his watch.

Readers can easily get involved in this tale as it will certainly call to mind many television and movie stories where the good guys must use their expertise to escape to safety from the evil pursuer. Grades 7-8

CHAPTER
EIGHT

# Realistic Fiction

Teen realistic fiction is teeming with contemporary stories based on real life situations. Often young protagonists face a plethora of social problems from date rape to death. In these novels, teenagers cope with social pressures from home and school. Readers witness characters struggling with drugs, pregnancies, disabilities, divorce, and bullying.

**Anderson, Laurie Halse.** *Prom.* New York: Viking, 2005.
Ashley Hannigan, a very ordinary student, becomes a reluctant heroine. She saves the high school prom in spite of the assistant principal and herself. Grades 6-8

**Anderson, Laurie Halse.** *Speak.* New York: Farrar Straus Giroux, 1999.
Only an art teacher seems to connect with high school freshman Melinda. She has chosen to be silent since a date rape incident because none of her former friends have forgiven her for calling 911 on a popular guy. Grades 6-8

**Coman, Carolyn.** *Many Stones.* Asheville: Front Street, 2000.
In a short but intense novel, Coman percolates the anger Berry Morgan feels toward her estranged father. The two travel to Johannesburg for a memorial service for her slain sister. Here the family's grieving is intensified amidst South Africa's own recent and painful history. Grade 8

**Fusco, Kimberly Newton.** *Tending to Grace.* New York: Alfred A. Knopf, 2004.
Cornelia Thornbill, a shy stuttering teenager, has been dumped by her mother at the home of Great-Aunt Agatha. Cornelia rediscovers herself by helping her illiterate aunt learn to read. Grades 7-8

**Holt, Kimberly Willis.** *My Louisiana Sky.* New York: Henry Holt and Co., Inc., 1998.
Holt's first novel tears at the heart. Tiger Ann deals with mentally slow parents, a grandmother's death, and a changing relationship with a male friend. Grades 6-7

**Holt, Kimberly Willis.** *When Zachary Beaver Came to Town.* New York: Holt, 1999.
Do you pay to see a 600-pound boy in a trailer? Sure you do, but 13-year-old Toby and his buddy, Cal, befriend Zachary Beaver, the deserted fat boy. Set in Texas in 1971, Toby is also worried about his brother who is fighting the war in Vietnam. Grades 6-7

**Howe, James.** *The Misfits.* New York: Atheneum Books for Young Readers, 2001.
All the students who feel left out may recognize themselves as a possible "misfit." James Howe wants his readers to know that bullying is bad and there should be room for all kinds of kids, whether totally independent, fat, strange, or gay. Grades 6-8

**Konigsburg, E. L.** *The Outcasts of 19 Schuyler Place.* New York: Atheneum Books for Young Readers, 2004.
We find Margaret at a horrible summer camp where she is bullied by other girls. She stoically refuses to participate until her eccentric uncles rescue her. Then she gets to rescue them! Grades 6-8

**Lord, Cynthia.** *Rules.* New York: Scholastic Press, 2006.
Catherine is frustrated with her autistic brother who she suspects prevents her from being accepted by girls her own age. A friendship with a paraplegic boy enables her to understand her own disconnect with special needs. Grades 6-7

**Myers, Walter Dean.** *Fallen Angels.* New York: Scholastic Inc., 1988.
The author used his own experience in Vietnam to write a gripping story of young soldiers in Vietnam. Readers will get a full description of the horrors of war. Grades 7-8

**Sones, Sonya.** *What My Mother Doesn't Know.* New York: Simon Pulse, 2003.
Teenage girls identify with Sophie who we meet in this verse novel. Sophie is in love with Dylan and, at the same time, emailing an unknown guy named Chaz. Girls devour this novel full of angst. Grades 6-8

**Williams-Garcia, Rita.** *Like Sisters on the Homefront.* New York: Lodestar Books, 1995.
When the novel opens, Gayle is pregnant for the second time. Mom sends her from the inner city to rural Georgia to gain respect for herself and her child. Grades 7-8

**Winerip, Michael.** *Adam Canfield and the Slash.* Cambridge: Candlewick Press, 2005.
This is the perfect middle school story for suburban students. Adam Canfield lives in a comfortable community where he is overbooked with school, lessons, and activities. While serving as co-editor of the school newspaper, he and his friend, Jennifer, expose a scandal involving the principal and manage to get the community on their side. This book is written with humor and style by a *New York Times* reporter. Grades 6-8

# CHAPTER NINE

# Science Fiction and Fantasy

Science fiction catapults the reader into the future. The future could look highly sophisticated with robots serving breakfast, or the future world may be primitive without electricity and lit only by candlelight. Science fiction may involve time travel, alternative civilizations, and other worlds.

Fantasy may be as simple as a redone fairy tale or a hero's quest to rescue civilization. These stories may have magical elements grounded in realism, or they may exist in an entirely original universe.

Science fiction and fantasy stories explore issues of good and evil in altered worlds, allowing authors to examine ethical questions untethered by common convention.

**Almond, David. *Skellig.*** New York: Delacorte Press, 1999.
Is he a bird, a man, a mythological creature? When Michael discovers Skellig in his garage, he cannot tell. He does, however, discover that he likes Chinese food. Grades 6-8

**Bradbury, Ray. *Fahrenheit 451.*** New York: Ballantine Books, 1953.
This classic published 50 years ago has withstood the test of time as it explores a futuristic fascist state where books are for burning. Grades 7-8

**Dickinson, Peter. *Eva.*** New York: Delacorte Press, 1989.
Eva is a beautiful young girl who awakens from a coma to find that her brain has been transferred to the head of a monkey. Grades 7-8

**DuPrau, Jeanne. *The City of Ember.*** New York: Random House, 2003.
Ember is a dystopia of darkness from which Lina and Doon must escape. Lina and Doon try to save the city as they search for the light. Grades 6-8

**Farmer, Nancy. *The Ear, the Eye, and the Arm.*** New York: Orchard Books, 1994.

Ear, Eye, and Arm are three mutant detectives doing their best to locate the kidnapped children of General Matsika. Science fiction and page-turning adventure kick in to make this novel unforgettable. Grade 6

**Farmer, Nancy. *The House of the Scorpion.*** New York: Atheneum Books for Young Readers, 2002.

In the land of Opium, somewhere between California and Mexico, is a country ruled by El Patron. This is the story of a young clone, Matteo Alacran, who plans to flee to escape his destiny. Grades 6-8

**Haddix, Margaret Peterson. *Among the Hidden.*** New York: Simon & Schuster Books for Young Readers, 1998.

Luke lives as a third child in a society where the Population Police allow a family to have only two children. When Luke discovers that there are other hidden children, he and Jen band together to try to overthrow the government. This is the first book in the Shadow Children series. Grades 6-8

**Hoeye, Michael. *Time Stops for No Mouse:*** *A Hermux Tantamoq Adventure.* New York: Putnam's, 2002.

What happens when glamorous Linka Perfinger bewitches a mild-mannered watchmaker, Hermux Tantamoq, and then disappears? Never mind that these characters are talking mice. What follows are many adventures that lead Hermux to the evil Doctor Mennus. Grades 6-7

**Ibbotson, Eva. *The Secret of Platform 13.*** New York: Dutton Children's Books, 1998.

Get aboard this fantasy ride to an enchanted island. Zany characters create humor and chaos as the king and queen plan to rescue their kidnapped son. Grade 6

**Nimmo, Jenny. *Midnight for Charlie Bone.*** New York: Orchard Books, 2003.

Charlie is "endowed," meaning he has a special talent. He can look at photographs, hear what was going on, and travel back in time. He is a descendant of the Red King and is sent to Bloor's Academy where he meets other endowed children. This book is the first in the series and Charlie will delight readers who love fantasy/adventure. Grades 6-7

**Philbrick, Rodman. *The Last Book in the Universe.*** New York: Blue Sky Press, 2000.

Spaz, an epileptic boy, lives in a society bereft of any vestige of cultured civilization. Searching for his foster sister, Bean, Spaz journeys with an old man, Ryter, to discover there is an Eden, but he is forced back to Urbia's toxic environment. Grades 7-8

**Pullman, Philip. *The Golden Compass.*** New York: Ballantine Books, 1997.

The Golden Compass is the first book of Pullman's Dark Materials trilogy. Lyra must travel to other fantasy worlds to rescue children who have been stolen. Readers are fascinated by this world where everyone has a daemon, a kind of animal that is both an extension of the soul and a protector as well. This is sophisticated high fantasy, much of it based on the work of John Milton. Grades 6-8

**Riordan, Rick.** *The Lightning Thief.* New York: Miramax/Hyperion, 2005.
Percy Jackson learns he is the son of the Greek god Poseidon, not just a kid with ADD. At Camp Half Blood, he begins a quest to retrieve Zeus' thunderbolt. This book is the first in the series, Percy Jackson & the Olympians. Grades 6-8

**Tolkien, J. R. R.** *The Fellowship of the Ring:* *Being the First Part of the Lord of the Rings.* Boston: Houghton Mifflin, 1954.
Tolkien writes quintessential high fantasy. Older readers will devour the Lord of the Rings trilogy that is set in the third age of Middle Earth. Grades 7-8

**Wrede, Patricia C.** *Dealing with Dragons.* San Diego: Harcourt Brace Jovanovich, 1990.
Princess Cimorene has had it! She's tired of life at court and wants out! This princess wants a life of excitement. She becomes the princess of the Dragon Kazul. Part of the Enchanted Forest chronicles and written with humor, this book will transport girls into a world of wizards and magic. Grade 6

# CHAPTER TEN

# Historical Fiction

This genre includes stories that are set in the past. Time and place dictate much of the action. Characters are fictionalized, but the events in the story give an accurate impression of an historical period. Authors do painstaking research to portray the events and culture of a time period from ancient civilizations to the twentieth century.

**Avi. *Crispin: The Cross of Lead.*** New York: Hyperion Books for Children, 2002.
Avi takes us to fourteenth century England and spins a tale about a young 13-year-old orphan who searches for his true identity. He is accused of murder and must outrun his enemies. Grade 6

**Beatty, Patricia. *Charley Skedaddle.*** Mahwah: Troll Associates, 1987.
Charley is a Bowery Boy who joins the Union Army. Because he is too young, he becomes a drummer boy. Overwhelmed by the death all about him, he deserts during a battle and comes of age on a farm with an old mountain woman who restores his courage. Grade 6

**Choldenko, Gennifer. *Al Capone Does My Shirts.*** New York: Scholastic, 2004.
Set in 1935, Choldenko's story features Moose Flanagan and his family who have moved to Alcatraz because his father was hired as the prison electrician. Moose copes with a new neighborhood with new friends in this unique setting. Moose's autistic sister, Natalie, complicates his life, but also illustrates his loyal and loving nature. Grades 6-7

**Cushman, Karen. *Rodzina.*** New York: Clarion Books, 2003.
Cushman, masterful historical storyteller, paints a picture of an orphan train in the 1880s. Central to the tale is Rodzina, a 12-year-old Polish orphan who is afraid she'll be sold into slavery. We travel from Chicago to California before Rodzina finally gets a home. Grades 6-7

**DeFelice, Cynthia C. The Apprenticeship of Lucas Whitaker.** New York: Farrar Straus Giroux, 1996.
When Lucas' family dies of tuberculosis, he leaves his home and travels to a nearby town in Connecticut to become a doctor's apprentice. Readers learn much about early medicine and what folks believed caused death and disease. Grades 6-8

**Jocelyn, Marthe.** *Mable Riley: A Reliable Record of Humdrum, Peril, and Romance.* Cambridge: Candlewick Press, 2004.

In 1901 Mable Riley learns about women's and workers' rights in Perth County, Ontario. With the book written in diary form, readers will warm to the heroine. Grades 6-7

**Ketchum, Liza.** *Where the Great Hawk Flies.* New York: Clarion Books, 2005.

Two young boys, one white and the other half Pequot Indian, are thrown together during the late 1700s. Hiram and Daniel come to understand each other and overcome inborn prejudices. Told with alternate points of view. Grades 6-7

**Levine, Gail Carson.** *Dave at Night.* New York: HarperCollins, 1999.

During the Depression, Dave is sent to a Jewish orphanage in Harlem, which Dickens might have envisioned. Dave is a survivor and escapes at night into the parties of the Harlem Renaissance. Based on Levine's grandfather's life story, readers will respond to the humor and action of the tale. Grade 6

**Morpurgo, Michael.** *Private Peaceful.* New York: Scholastic, 2006.

Michael Morpurgo, in the voice of 18-year-old Thomas Peaceful, tells a bittersweet story of brothers during WWI. One brother will be sacrificed at dawn for cowardice. Readers will know the truth of the events and will grieve for all who died nobly fighting in the trenches. Grades 6-8

**Myers, Walter Dean.** *The Journal of Scott Pendleton Collins: A World War II Soldier.* New York: Scholastic, 1999.

Part of the Dear America series, this is a good title to give students who will ask for another book like Fallen Angels. A young soldier experiences an allied offensive attack on Omaha Beach. The young soldier matures into an adult as a result of the battlefield. Grades 6-7

**Napoli, Donna Jo.** *Stones in Water.* New York: Dutton Children's Books, 1997.

Italian Roberto and his Jewish friend, Samuele, are rounded up at the movies and sent to a Nazi work camp. Roberto will eventually escape to Russia and survive in the frozen Ukraine. Grades 6-7

**O'Dell, Scott.** *Sarah Bishop.* Boston: Houghton Mifflin, 1980.

Sarah Bishop chooses to survive in the wilderness after harrowing events during the American Revolutionary War. As a woman alone, she must be careful not to suggest she is a witch. Grades 6-7

**Rees, Celia.** *Witch Child.* Cambridge: Candlewick Press, 2000.

Mary Nuttall lives in Puritan Massachusetts after leaving England where her grandmother was hung as a witch. The author takes a different approach here, as Mary really is a pagan witch in a community looking for signs of witchcraft. Grades 7-8

**Westall, Robert.** *The Kingdom by the Sea.* New York: Farrar Straus Giroux, 1991.

Harry somehow survives after his home is destroyed during a London bombing. Taking the family documents and a few blankets, he runs away from London in order to avoid being placed with a disagreeable cousin. He becomes friends with a stray dog and together they take on adversity. A surprise ending will startle the reader. Grades 6-7

# Mysteries

Everyone loves a mystery. Mystery books are plot driven, offering up puzzling questions and secret actions. Students who voraciously read Nancy Drew and Encyclopedia Brown in elementary school will be searching for new page-turners. Middle school mystery authors like Lois Duncan and Caroline Cooney await. Young detectives like Sammy Keyes investigate chilling events. Teenage protagonists often solve the case without parental assistance. After all, aren't these young adult books?

**Abrahams, Peter. *Down the Rabbit Hole.*** New York: Laura Geringer Books, 2005.
Adult mystery writer Peter Abrahams' first YA novel introduces eighth grader Ingrid Levin-Hill, an avid Sherlock Holmes fan. Emulating her fictional detective idol, Ingrid solves the cracked-up Katie case and introduces the Echo Falls series. Grades 6-8

**Avi. *Wolf Rider: A Tale of Terror.*** New York: Aladdin Paperbacks, 1986.
Avi's 20-year-old mystery still pleases the crowd. When 15-year-old Andy Sadowski gets a crank phone call indicating that a murder has occurred, he finds that, like crying wolf, no one believes him. Grades 6-7

**Christie, Agatha. *And Then There Were None.*** New York: Berkley Books, 1991.
Agatha Christie's adult classic still fascinates today's YA readers. Drawing from the "Ten Little Indians" nursery rhyme, she sets up a traditional gathering of characters, only to have each one die one at a time. Grade 8

**Cooney, Caroline B. *The Face on the Milk Carton.*** New York: Bantam Doubleday Dell, 1994.
Romance and mystery coincide in this compelling read. Janie recognizes her face on a milk carton and realizes she is not living with her actual parents. This is the first book in the Janie Johnson series. Grades 6-8

**Duncan, Lois. *Killing Mr. Griffin.*** Boston: Little, Brown & Company, 1978.
For almost 30 years, students have chosen this kidnapping gone wrong novel. When the English teacher accidentally dies in the midst of a grim student prank to scare him, the teenagers must face the consequences. Grades 7-8

**Ehrlich, Amy. *Joyride.*** Cambridge: Candlewick Press, 2001.

Poor Nina Lewis is forced to move many times from coast to coast. Nina will eventually discover the chilling secret her mother has kept hidden for a long time.

**Hiassen, Carl. *Hoot.*** New York: Knopf, 2002.

Adult writer Carl Hiaasen's first YA novel is set in Florida. Roy Eberhardt, new kid in town, bands together with outsider Mullet Fingers, to stop construction of Mother Paula's Pancake House on a site inhabited by young burrowing owls. Plenty of humor, fun characters, and a well-constructed plot make an exciting story. Grades 6-8

**Raskin, Ellen. *The Westing Game.*** New York: E. P. Dutton, 1978.

Raskin sets up the classic closed group mystery that uncovers the clues to the inheritance of eccentric millionaire Sam Westing. Grade 6

**Updale, Eleanor. *Montmorency: Thief, Liar, Gentleman?*** New York: Orchard Books, 2005.

Once Montmorency escapes from prison and assumes a double identity, he lives two lives, one as a gentleman and the other as a thief who uses the London sewer system in early Victorian London. The first in a series, readers will want to read all. Grades 6-8

**Windsor, Patricia. *The Christmas Killer.*** New York: Scholastic, 1991.

In a small town in Connecticut, Rose gets psychic messages from the dead that help police to find the next murdered teenage girl. Grade 8

# CHAPTER TWELVE

# Multicultural Fiction

Multicultural books break down barriers and celebrate diversity by reflecting differences among ethnic groups. By making connections, these books help students to see the world and other cultures in a new way. Differences become a source of strength, not division. Students learn about other cultures, destroying misconceptions. Books may be set in other lands or culturally mirror a part of our own society. Some titles are historical fiction and others present authentic pictures of ethnic groups.

**Curtis, Christopher Paul. *Bud, Not Buddy.*** New York: Delacorte Press, 1999.
During the Depression, 10-year-old Bud, an African-American orphan, searches out his father only to discover his grandfather, a jazz musician. Bud's outlook on life is both philosophical and humorous and carries the reader through the action-packed plot. Grade 6

**Joseph, Lynn. *The Color of My Words.*** New York: Joanna Cotler Books, 2000.
Set in the Dominican Republic, 12-year-old Ana, a writer in the making, watches as her brother fights against the repressive government. Ana needs words to describe her grief when her brother is killed. Grade 6

**Laird, Elizabeth. *Kiss the Dust.*** New York: Dutton Children's Books, 1992.
Thirteen-year-old Tara and her family are Kurdish refugees escaping from Iraq. Laird describes a family faced with terrible life-threatening situations before they get safe passage to England. Grades 7-8

**Namioka, Lensey. *Ties That Bind, Ties That Break.*** New York: Delacorte Press, 1999.
Ailin challenges Chinese culture by refusing to bind her feet. Grades 6-7

**Osborne, Mary Pope. *Adaline Falling Star.*** New York: Scholastic, 2000.
Adaline, the daughter of Kit Carson and an Arapaho Indian woman, is sent to live with prejudicial relatives who treat her like a slave. She escapes to search for her father. Along the way, she is befriended by an abandoned dog until her journey ends. Grades 6-7

**Paulsen, Gary. *The Crossing.*** New York, NY: Orchard Books, 1987.

Manny is a street kid in Juarez, Mexico, who desperately wants to cross the border into Texas. A chance meeting with a drunken U.S. sergeant changes their lives. Grades 6-8

**Perkins, Mitali. *The Not-So-Star-Spangled Life of Sunita Sen.*** New York: Little, Brown, 2005.

A young Indian girl has trouble dealing with cultural issues. She finds her Indian-American parents hypocritical when they over-please her grandparents on a visit to their home in California. Grades 7-8

**Ryan, Pam Munoz. *Esperanza Rising.*** New York: Scholastic Press, 2000.

In this novel, the heroine goes from riches to rags when pampered and entitled Esperanza must flee Mexico with her mother and former servant and live in California as a migrant worker. Esperanza, because of hardships faced, transforms into a caring and humane adult. Grade 6

**Spinelli, Jerry. *Maniac Magee.*** Boston: Little, Brown, 1990.

In the popular modern tall tale about a homeless boy who becomes a legend in town, Spinelli explores racism and friendship while allowing Maniac to bridge the gap between whites and blacks. Grade 6

**Staples, Suzanne Fisher. *Dangerous Skies.*** New York: Farrar, Straus, and Giroux, 1996.

Suzanne Fisher Staples never paints a black and white picture. Her fiction rings true in shades of gray. In this novel Buck Smith and his black friend, Tunes, learn about racism in their own small Chesapeake Bay community. Grades 6-7

**Staples, Suzanne Fisher. *Shabanu: Daughter of the Wind.*** New York: Knopf, 1999.

Shabanu is a heart-wrenching story of a young Pakistani girl who lives with her nomadic family in the Cholistan desert. Life is cruel and tough, but somehow Shabanu keeps happiness in her heart until faced with an unwanted fate: an arranged marriage to a man she does not love. Grades 7-8

**Whelan, Gloria. *Homeless Bird.*** New York: HarperCollins, 2000.

Koly, who is only 13 and a widow, is rejected by her husband's family and left in the city of Vrinda-van by her merciless mother-in-law. Grades 6-7

# Sports Fiction

Teenagers enjoy reading books on topics of interest to them. Students are often involved in a variety of sports at the middle school level. By providing fiction titles with sports themes, readers will be absorbed in the stories. This genre is quite appealing to reluctant readers or simply readers who are crazy about sports.

The following books have sports themes, but stand out as well-written novels that tackle additional issues. They are engaging because they're not just about sports.

**Bloor, Edward. *Tangerine.*** San Diego: Harcourt Brace, 1997.

There is something here for both soccer and softball fans. When the Fisher family moves to Florida, not only is there plenty of sports action, but also the mystery surrounding Paul's near blindness is revealed. Grades 7-8

**Deuker, Carl. *Night Hoops.*** Boston: Houghton Mifflin, 2000.

Male students will relate to the narrator, Nick Abbott, who dreams of being a basketball star. Playing hoops at night with his neighbor, Trent Dawson, Nick learns about the game and many of his personal problems. Grades 7-8

**Feinstein, John. *Last Shot: A Final Four Mystery.*** New York: Knopf, 2005.

Feinstein delivers mystery and adventure to the Final Four tournament. Two eighth graders, a boy and a girl, win a writing contest and are sent to cover the event. They discover a star player is being blackmailed to throw the game, and they set about rescuing him and the tournament. Grades 6-8

**Gutman, Dan. *Shoeless Joe & Me: A Baseball Card Adventure.*** New York: Scholastic Inc., 2004.

Gutman's series on baseball card adventures transports the main character and the reader back in time. In this adventure, Joe Stoshack travels back to 1919 to meet Shoeless Joe and learn about the Black Sox Scandal. Male readers will gravitate to Gutman's other titles. Grade 6

**Klass, David. *Danger Zone*.** New York: Scholastic, 1996.

This novel is a terrific basketball story, but also manages to play out all the myths and realities around racism within American culture. When a white rural teenager joins a high school dream team and encounters slick black guys from L.A., we witness a poignant clash of culture. Grades 6-8

**Lee, Marie G. *Necessary Roughness*.** New York: HarperTrophy, 1998.

Marie Lee's novel is an excellent companion to Danger Zone. This novel moves 16-year-old Korean American, Chan, from L.A. to rural Minnesota. Chan and his twin sister are outsiders and face bigotry. Their plight is made more complicated by their father who is culturally bound in Korean tradition and refuses to become Americanized. Lots of football action will satisfy sports fans. Grades 7-8

**Lupica, Mike. *Travel Team*.** New York: Philomel Books, 2004.

Twelve-year-old Danny Walker has been cut from the basketball team because he is too short. His divorced dad rescues him by starting another team peppered with other players that had been rejected. Circumstances set Danny to coach the team to a culminating win. Grades 6-8

**Lynch, Chris. *Gold Dust*.** New York: HarperCollins, 2000.

Chris Lynch takes the friendship of a black Dominican and a baseball-crazy white American and sets it against the racial tensions of the busing era in 1970's Boston. Both boys share baseball, but the racially charged atmosphere destroys their close ties. Grades 6-7

**Lynch, Chris. *Slot Machine*.** New York: HarperCollins Publishers, 1995.

*Slot Machine* is a hilarious laugh-out-loud tale. Overweight Elvin Bishop is sent to sports camp. He goes there with two friends, but it is the last place he wants to be. Elvin has huge difficulty finding any sport he likes, but eventually he settles on wrestling. Lynch writes with such humor, the reader may forget how dreadful this camp actually is. Grade 8

**Mackel, Kathy. *MadCat*.** New York: HarperCollins, 2005.

MadCat, a terrific pitcher on her local team, competes in the softball nationals. In this novel, girls will witness female athletes who are talented and want to win but discover the cost of climbing their way to the top. Grades 6-8

CHAPTER
**FOURTEEN**

# *Biography and Nonfiction*

Spellbinding biographies or memoirs captivate young readers. Courage shown or obstacles overcome by struggling heroes or heroines will resonate with today's teenagers. Previously mentioned in the chapter on Booked Conversation, *In My Hands, The Glass Castle,* and *Hole in My Life* exemplify this style of book.

Still others will enjoy reading about history, early medicine, sports, or freakish science. Readers seeking information, ideas, and true stories will gravitate to this genre. Authentic renderings of the strange and fascinating such as *Phineas Gage: A Gruesome but True Story about Brain Science* will appeal to those who prefer nonfiction to fiction.

**Anonymous. *Annie's Baby: The Diary of Anonymous, a Pregnant Teenager.*** New York: Avon Books, 2005.

Impressionable 14-year-old Annie finds herself pregnant. She gets love and support from her mother when she decides to keep the baby. Sadly Annie learns that the task is beyond her ability and she must give up her baby for adoption. Grades 6-8

**Cox, Clinton. *Houdini: Master of Illusion.*** New York: Scholastic Press, 2001.

Cox's well-researched book relates the life story of Ehrich Weiss who renamed himself Harry Houdini and became a world famous magician. Cox describes many of Houdini's magic feats and ushers us into his personal life story. Grades 6-8

**Dahl, Roald. Boy: *Tales of Childhood.*** New York: Farrar, Straus, Giroux, 1984.

Students who grew up reading Roald Dahl's amusing stories will not be disappointed with his autobiographical sketch. The same charm and diabolical humor that permeate his tales also pervade this lighthearted life story. Grades 6-7

**Duncan, Lois.** *Who Killed My Daughter?* New York: Dell Publishing, 1994.

Readers of Lois Duncan's popular mysteries will be drawn to this true unsolved crime story. Duncan's daughter was murdered in Albuquerque, New Mexico. She was found dead in her car, slumped over the steering wheel. Police believed that her death was a result of a random shooting, but the author took the case to the FBI for further investigation. Lois Duncan consulted psychics, but the crime remains unsolved. Her heartbreaking story rings with irony. Grades 7-8

**Filipovic, Zlata.** *Zlata's Diary: A Child's Life in Sarajevo.* New York: Viking, 1994.

Zlata is a school girl in Bosnia who kept a diary. She is a happy girl who is forced to cope with the tragic events of the Balkan conflict. Zlata's observations will enlighten young readers to the tragedy of war and personal loss. Grade 6

**Fleischman, John.** *Phineas Gage: A Gruesome but True Story about Brain Science.* Boston: Houghton Mifflin, 2002.

Imagine living for 20 years with a hole in your head that you received from a 13-pound iron rod. Author John Fleischman tells the true story of Phineas Gage's accident, incorporating scientific facts on brain science to enhance the story and satisfy the curious. Grades 6-7

**Gottlieb, Lori.** *Stick Figure: A Diary of My Former Self.* New York: Simon & Schuster, 2000.

In this memoir, Gottlieb chronicles her teenage struggle with anorexia. When she was 11, she became obsessed with dieting, hoping to exercise some control over her life. Instead her parents must hospitalize her when she almost dies. After reading this book, students will be compelled to think about issues around body image. Grades 6-8

**Grogan, John.** *Marley & Me: Life and Love with the World's Worst Dog.* New York: Morrow, 2005.

An adult best seller, John Grogan's memoir about life with a naughty yellow lab attracts teen readers as well. Marley might be the worst behaved dog of all time, but he is irresistible. Grogan touches the hearts of his readers who sympathize with the bad dog issues, but fall in love with this canine in spite of it all. Grades 6-8

**Macy, Sue.** *A Whole New Ball Game: The Story of the All-American Girls Professional Baseball League.* New York: Puffin Books, 1995.

During WWII, a female professional baseball team was established. Author Sue Macy provides an engrossing story of pioneering female athletes. The cover photo with women wearing cheerleader style apparel sets the tone for understanding the strides women have made in sports. Grades 6-8

**Myers, Walter Dean.** *The Greatest: Muhammad Ali.* New York: Scholastic Inc., 2001.

Walter Dean Myers brings the story of Cassius Clay, the man who became Muhammad Ali, to life. Not only do we learn about Ali's rise to heavyweight champion, but also his decision not to go to Vietnam. Myers admires Ali and portrays life in the boxing ring. Grades 6-8

**O'Grady, Scott.** *Basher Five-Two: The True Story of F-16 Fighter Pilot Captain Scott O'Grady.* New York: Doubleday, 1997.

Students who choose survival fiction will appreciate this true survival tale about Captain Scott O'Grady. He relates his ordeal when his airplane was shot down in enemy territory. This extraordinary circumstance made him a hero and serves as a tribute to this strength of character. Grades 6-8

# Index of Authors and Titles